DISCUSSIONS OF LITERATURE

discussions of

modern american drama

Edited with an Introduction by
WALTER J. MESERVE, The University of Kansas

D. C. HEATH AND COMPANY
BOSTON

For
A. C. Edwards
Founder and Editor of *Modern Drama*

CONTENTS

PLAYWRIGHTS

INTRODUCTION

George Jean Nathan once declared that there are two classes of men: those who like vaudeville and those who can stand it when they are drunk. A number of literary critics take a similar view of American drama written before World War I, and only a relatively few serious critics have been attracted by American plays or by the developing trends in American drama. Only three historical studies, for example, exist — Montrose J. Moses, *The American Dramatist*, rev. 1925; Margaret Mayorga, *A Short History of the American Drama*, 1932; Arthur Hobson Quinn, *A History of the American Drama from the Beginning to the Civil War*, rev. 1943; and *A History of the American Drama from the Civil War to the Present Day*, rev. 1936 — and all are now dated and inadequate. More recently Alan S. Downer briefly surveyed *Fifty Years of American Drama 1900–1950*, and Joseph Wood Krutch attempted an assessment of *American Drama Since 1918* in 1939. In 1957 Krutch added a "Postwar" chapter, and in 1962 Gerald Weales presented *American Drama Since World War II*. The overwhelming tendency of most critics of the drama and theater, however, has been to consider only those plays which they viewed in production. Although G. B. Shaw once answered a critic who complained about the condition of the theater by noting that the drama was *always* at a low ebb, American critics have generally found joy only in their contemporary theater — with the consequent loss of interest in drama as literature or in a developing American drama.

That American dramatic criticism has been generally undistinguished is a fact that cannot be escaped. Although before World War I this fact may be explained in terms of the mainly uninspired American plays, one must obviously seek other reasons for more recent years. The journalistic approach, the limited demands of the critic's audience, the accustomed apathy of literary critics toward American drama — these are some of the answers. A large percentage of dramatic criticism has been produced by journalistic reviewers haunted by deadlines and the blue pencils of their editors. Before the turn of the century these critics were either paid "puffers" or reporters who might be asked to cover a fire one moment and a drama the next. Such critics, of course, gradually disappeared. Not until the 1920's, however, were reporters generally replaced by critics with some education and sensitivity. Even today good critical essays on American drama which treat more than a single performance of a play are not common. The tendency among reviewing critics has been to emphasize the production of the play and to discuss the evening's entertainment. This position is well stated by William Hawkins, drama critic for the New York *Telegram* and *Sun,* who noted (*Theatre Annal,* XIV, 1956), "that the bulk of the critics' readers are interested in a simple, blanket opinion which makes clear the subject of the show and its overall quality. They do not want their limited reading time cluttered up with complex or erudite explanations or comparisons." Among literary or academic critics few have discussed the drama as literature, and fewer have enjoyed either the interest or the background to assess the movements in American drama. Until quite recently criticism of plays has been generally left to the drama or theater critics of newspapers or weekly periodicals who have, for their purposes, provided a satisfactory criticism. But dramatic criticism as a literary art has been seriously neglected.

There is emerging today, however, a new emphasis in American dramatic criticism. It is the purpose of this volume to present in chronological sequence those essays which most effectively evaluate some of the major aspects and the principal dramatists of modern American drama. Excerpts from John Corbin and A. H. Quinn suggest an early type of criticism as well as the scope of modern American drama. Distinctive approaches to the writing of plays are clear in the excerpt from the early and quite revolutionary essay by James A. Herne and in the later essays of O'Neill and Albee, among others.

The beginnings of *modern* American drama, however, present a problem. William Archer, the English critic, once wrote that for these beginnings one should look on the shores of Cape Cod in 1915 where the Provincetown Players first met. One might, with equal logic, suggest an earlier date. When Ibsen started writing plays in 1850, American drama was still firmly rooted in the romantic tradition of early 19th century Europe. While Ibsen, Shaw, and Strindberg were producing their masterpieces of modern drama near the end of the century, American playgoers were still watching the melodrama of Augustin Daly, the farces of Charles Hoyt, and the romances of David Belasco; and when Ibsen's most serious imitator in America, James A. Herne, produced *Margaret Fleming* in 1890, most theatergoers were offended by the play's frankness. Change, however, was imminent. Herne prescribed it in his essay on "Art for Truth's Sake in the Drama," and John Corbin recognized it in his essay "The Dawn of American Drama" — a dawn which emerged before World War I with the plays of William Vaughn Moody, Rachel Crothers, Edward Sheldon, and Charles Rann Kennedy. Although relatively few plays before World War I show such daring as Herne's *Margaret Fleming,* the beginnings of modern American drama had been made. The next step would be the production of the plays of Eugene O'Neill whose search for meaning in a new form marks America's full scale arrival into the modern drama of western civilization.

From 1890 until 1915 a few critics saw changes taking place in American drama. Alfred Hennequin in "Characteristics of American Drama [*Arena,* I (May, 1890), 700–709] declared that the French melodrama and the English melodrama had combined to produce a new type of American play — the social melodrama. Progress for this kind of play, however, was slow because theater managers felt an antipathy toward it among audiences and because critics like Clayton Hamilton ["Melodrama, Old and New," *Bookman,* XXXIII (May, 1911), 309–314] resented a change which presented a "new species of melodrama that is ashamed of itself" as it takes the form of "a serious study of contemporary social problems." The better critics — Walter P. Eaton, Brander Matthews — saw the change and applauded it, but the condition of American drama and dramatic criticism remained one of unstable transition.

With the production of a more sophisticated and penetrating drama after World War I there emerged a more cosmopolitan and educated criticism. During these years the enthusiastic and indefatigable Arthur Hobson Quinn was teaching courses in American drama at the University of Pennsylvania and by 1924 could survey the plays being produced and the dramatists in an essay entitled "Modern American Drama." Jesse Lynch Williams' *Why Marry?* had been awarded the first Pulitzer Prize for drama in 1917, and numerous plays were being acted as the Little Theatres continued their fight with Broadway. Before the Crash of 1929 most of America's playwrights of the 1920–1940 period had written plays — Paul Green, Marc Connelly, Philip Barry, George Kelly, John Howard Lawson, Elmer Rice, Sidney Howard, S. N. Behrman, Robert Sherwood. Although there were many reviewers of their plays, there were very few serious critics — Montrose Moses, A. H. Quinn, Barrett Clark. Perhaps literary critics had to muse over the situation for a few more years before they realized that American drama offered a challenge to their sensibilities.

Toward the end of the 1930's, however, a challenge was recognized. A major activity of the decade, of course, was the left-wing drama, most carefully reviewed in such places as *The Daily Worker* and *New Masses.* Some left-wing dramatists, such as John Howard Lawson and Albert Matz, wrote both plays and criticism. Harold Clurman, a critic and director, later assessed the effect of the most significant acting group of the thirties — Group Theatre — in *The Fervent Years*, 1945; and Eleanor Flexner emphasized her left-wing views in *American Playwrights*, 1918–1939. Other plays stimulated a more liberal and sometimes academic if not a more serious criticism. Younger professors such as Joseph Wood Krutch, Lionel Trilling, and Joseph Mersand began to follow the lead of Quinn and Clark. Although drama critics for the newspapers and magazines continued to provide most of the criticism — George Jean Nathan, Alexander Woollcott, John Mason Brown, Rosamond Gilder, Brooks Atkinson — there was an emphasis on more thought-provoking criticisms by the mid-1940's, which were enlivened by the astute observations of critics such as Mary McCarthy, Edith Isaacs, and Edmund Wilson. But essays of substance and quality appeared very seldom: a tradition of scholarly dramatic criticism was yet to be established.

Such a tradition is, in fact, only now getting underway. Contemporary professional critics and many with academic background, like their counterparts before World War II, most frequently consider only a particular production of a play, an analysis of a play, or perhaps the work of a certain playwright, but almost never the contributions of the playwright to American or world drama or the more subtle aspects of his art. Many critics — even those who have attempted an historical approach — lack a substantial background in drama which would enable them to make critical judgments on the drama as a whole. But evidence of a more serious and literary criticism is slowly becoming more discernible. Courses in American drama are being added to college and university curricula. Distinguished journals such as *Modern Drama, The Tulane Drama Review,* and *Drama Survey* are beginning to appear. A scholarly concern for American drama is at last becoming respectable.

A critically intelligent view of the various aspects of modern American drama is still very difficult to present, however, because most critics writing substantial essays on American drama mainly confine their studies to Eugene O'Neill or to some aspect of the drama since World War II. Yet the challenge of modern America drama as a whole is being more widely recognized and accepted; its "intrusion" into world drama has been accomplished; and a tradition of scholarly criticism is being established. The essays in this collection suggest the beginnings and the progress of that tradition.

WALTER J. MESERVE

notes on the
CONTRIBUTORS

john corbin (1870–1959) was a drama critic and editor, mainly on the staff of the New York *Times*.

arthur hobson quinn (1875–1960) late professor at the University of Pennsylvania, wrote the most complete history of American drama: *American Drama from the Beginning to the Civil War* (1943) and . . . *Civil War to the Present Day* (1936).

walter j. meserve is Professor of English at the University of Kansas. He is an associate editor of *Modern Drama* and has edited *The Complete Plays of W. D. Howells* (1960).

lionel trilling is well-known for his contributions to modern criticism. Among his books are *The Liberal Imagination* (1950) and *A Gathering of Fugitives* (1956).

harold clurman, director and dramatic critic, was a founder of the Group Theatre (1931–1941). He is the author of numerous critical articles and *The Fervent Years* (1945).

donna gerstenberger teaches English at the University of Washington. She has published critical essays on the drama and is co-author with George Hendrick of *The American Novel 1789–1959: A Checklist of Twentieth Century Criticism* (1961).

edith j. r. isaacs (1878–1956) made her career as an editor, mainly with the *Theatre Arts Monthly* (1924–1946). Her publications include *The Negro in the American Theatre* (1947).

travis m. bogard teaches in the Department of Dramatic Arts at the University of California. His interests in Elizabethan drama and modern British and American drama have resulted in critical essays and his book *The Tragic Satire of John Webster,* 1955.

joseph wood krutch has retired as Professor of Dramatic Literature at Columbia University. Among his numerous critical works is *The American Drama Since 1918* (rev. 1957).

laurence kitchin is an English dramatic critic who publishes in *The Times* and *The Observer*. In 1960 he wrote a survey of the English theatre entitled *Mid-Century Drama*.

robert brustein, associate Professor of English at Columbia University, is drama critic for *The New Republic*. His *Theatre of Revolt* was published in 1964.

edd winfield parks is Professor of English at the University of Georgia. His publications include periodical criticism and *Anti-Bellum Southern Literary Critics* (1962).

thomas f. driver, an Associate Professor at Union Theological Seminary, has published critical essays and *The Sense of History in Greek and Shakespearean Drama* (1960); he is co-editor of *Poems of Belief and Doubt* (1964).

mary mc carthy, one of America's best known writers, was theater critic for the *Partisan Review* from 1937–1948. Her collected dramatic criticism was published in 1963.

james a. herne (1839–1901) was an actor, manager, and dramatist (*Margaret Fleming*, 1890) who attempted to raise the drama to the realistic level demanded by W. D. Howells.

owen davis (1874–1956), one of the most successful writers of American melodramatic thrillers, turned to serious drama before World War I and received a Pulitzer Prize for *Icebound* in 1923.

eugene o'neill (1888–1953), America's most distinguished dramatist, was awarded three Pulitzer Prizes and won the Nobel Prize for Literature in 1936.

maxwell anderson (1888–1959) is best remembered for his attempt to bring poetry to the theater in *Elizabeth the Queen* (1930) and *Winterset* (1935).

tennessee williams is the well-known dramatist whose plays include *The Glass Menagerie* (1944), *A Streetcar Named Desire* (1947) and *Camino Real* (1953).

arthur miller has a serious interest in the social aspect of modern tragedy which he treats in essays and in such plays as *Death of a Salesman* (1949) and *The Crucible* (1953).

edward albee is recognized as America's foremost contributor to the avant-garde drama. Among his best known plays are "The Sandbox" (1959), a one-act play, *Who's Afraid of Virginia Woolf* (1962), and *Tiny Alice* (1965).

john corbin

THE DAWN OF
THE AMERICAN DRAMA

In an article on "The Twilight of the Poets," the sad purport of which was poetically adumbrated in its title, Mr. Edmund Clarence Stedman once remarked, "The time has come for poetry in any form that shall be *dramatic.* . . . I think that our future efforts will result in dramatic verse, and even in actual dramas for both the closet and the stage." This he gave forth, not as a prophecy, but as a speculation, founded on certain general tendencies in our life. "We scarcely can forecast next month's weather from the numberless shifting currents of to-day," he admitted; and he further safeguarded himself by saying, "I am aware that this belief has been entertained before, and prematurely; it was strong in the time of Taylor, Dunlap and Payne. Nor would our own experiments be much more significant than theirs, were it not for the recent and encouraging efforts of our younger authors, many of whom are among the poets already named." . . . Quite boldly, then, I prophesy the dawn of the American drama; and quite confidently, too, for the drama has already dawned. . . .

The nature of the theatrical trust, the so-called syndicate, is pretty well known though I am inclined to think that its character has been somewhat unduly blackened. Its purpose is frankly commercial. To berate it for its lack of altruistic devotion to the art of the drama is as illogical and as perverse as it would be to berate publishers because they do not endow libraries, or picture dealers because they fail to give their wares to the art museums. In a people who, of all moderns, have most stolidly refused to organize in behalf of the greatest of all arts, the cry that private merchants have cast the drama to the dogs is grotesquely comic. Two great services the commercial managers have rendered us; they have raised the calling of playwright and actor to a stable and lucrative vocation, and they have familiarized the entire continent with many of the best works of the dramatists of Europe. It has often been pointed

From *The Atlantic Monthly*, XCIV (May, 1907), 632–644. Copyright 1907, by The Atlantic Monthly Company, Boston 16, Mass. Reprinted by permission of the publisher.

out that the most powerful stimulus to artistic creation has been famil-
iarity with the more advanced products of other lands and peoples. The
work of the syndicate in this direction, though partial and unconscious,
has been powerful and fruitful. [One] result has been to develop a
body of playwrights who may be called the syndicate school. . . .

The plays of Bronson Howard are still performed on the humble
stages of local stock companies. All of them are instinct with broad
and wholesome human sympathy and racy masculine humor. One of
them, *The Henrietta,* held the regular stage until the recent death of
Stuart Robson. The earliest of our most characteristic genre of plays, the
business play, it is still the ablest, excelling alike in its appeal to vigorous
emotion and in its grasp of salient, humorous character. When it was
first produced it was censured, somewhat academically, perhaps, for presenting on the same stage, farcical comedy and melodramatic death. A
more valid objection is that its moral values are mixed. We are expected
to laugh, and in fact do laugh, with the Wall Street buccaneer who,
betraying a widow's trust in him, deliberately brings financial ruin on her
in order to force her to marry him; and at the same time we are called
upon to exult, and do exult, in the death of his son, who has been similarly treacherous to his father. Behold the triumph of dexterously ma-
nipulated values! The least to be said of this is that the play, in spite of
its indubitable power, belongs to a dramatic convention — that of the
Victorian era — which is radically false and factitious. . . .

[Contemporary] syndicate playwrights, meanwhile, have shown a
tendency to exhaustion not unlike that of the English school with which
their development synchronized. Mr. Gillette's *Clarice*, his only original
play in a decade, opened with an act of delicious sentimental comedy,
but after that declined into unpleasant and incredible melodrama.
Mr. Thomas has for two years produced only actor vehicles; they have
had a full measure of his racy wit, but have been otherwise without
originality or strength. It must be added, however, that his powers have
always been subject to lapses of considerable duration.

Mr. Fitch's case is problematical in the extreme. From the days
when, as a youth, he wrote *Beau Brummell*, it has been evident that he
is gifted with a freshness of observation, a spontaneous fecundity of
invention, and a skill in the externals of the art of the theatre that are
truly phenomenal. Both in drama and in comedy, he has written scenes
and characters which are at once more original, more varied, and of a
higher quality than the work of any of his competitors. A considerable
proportion of his extraordinarily copious output has been ill conceived,
though never without touches of originality; but his successes have been
equally numerous, and whenever, as not infrequently happens, one of
them is revived, — as for example such dissimilar pieces as *The Climbers*

and *Captain Jinks,* — its vitality and vivacity are found to be impaired. And his powers are apparently still in the ascendant.

What he lacks is a feeling for the deeper emotional and spiritual themes of life, and the mental grasp necessary to work his subject out with sustained and symmetrical technique. Twice of late he has given hopeful evidence of an ability to rise above his previous limitations, in *The Girl with the Green Eyes,* and *The Truth.* Neither play treats a theme comparable in depth or in scope with the themes of the best plays of the leading English playwrights, to say nothing of the intellectual dramatists of the Continent. Jealousy is the ugliest and least dignified of the passions, and habitual lying is at best a vice. None the less, Jinny, the girl with the green eyes, stands forth as one of the most individual, vivacious, and poignant characters of the contemporary stage; and though the play as a whole turns upon a rather factitious complication and ends in sheer bathos, it has one entire act, the third, of quite masterly salience and power. . . .

No part of Mr. Stedman's speculation has been more accurately fulfilled than that the great inspiration to our drama would come from our younger poets — though Mr. William Vaughn Moody and Mr. Percy MacKaye are of a very different vintage from the poets he had in mind. Mr. Moody has produced a prose play, and Mr. MacKaye a play in verse, which challenge comparison with the best work of the modern stage in any country.

In the first enthusiasm over *The Great Divide,* . . . the temptation was strong to proclaim it as marking definitely the opening of a new and triumphant epoch. Here was a play on a vital and permanent theme, and wrought out with a skill which, though it was by no means masterly and sometimes fell short of unmistakable clarity, was in the main as strongly dramatic as literary. Beside it the cleverness and mirth of our previous best, its satire, its morality and its sentiment, somehow seemed to shrink. . . . The significant fact is that in *The Great Divide* Mr. Moody has found his true self both in his manner and his matter. He writes as only he can write or has written; and his message, as it somewhat strangely happens, is the direct reverse of that of his earlier poems. Without being in the least political, his play is essentially imperialistic; it is a deep and convincing presentation of the right of sturdy might, however crude and tyrannous, in opposition to the thin and anemic self-righteousness of our traditional puritanism.

The "great divide" of the title is the line of demarcation between the West of primitive impulse and the East of refined and conscious propriety. Originally the play was called *The Sabine Woman,* in reference to the fact that the hero lays hands of violence upon the heroine and forces her to submit to his will. Three drunken roisterers come upon

Ruth Jordan, left alone for the night on a ranch. The best of them, an American named Ghent, shoots up one greaser and buys off another with a chain of nuggets from his neck; and as the price of protecting Ruth from outrage he leads her to the nearest magistrate. . . .

It would be hard to overestimate the originality or value of such a treatment of such a theme. The wages of sin, so our preachers and playwrights are accustomed to tell us, are death; the reward of sorrow and wrong new strength to the soul. Here is a dramatist who shows us that the wages of sin may be a purer life, that sorrow and wrong may corrupt. Ruth's sternly puritan brother, when he learns of the manner in which Ghent won her, has the impulse to kill him. Her mother, who is a model of conventional goodness, says, "You should have killed yourself!" Ruth has learned that either course would have meant the loss of all life has to give. . . . In one element of success, it seems to me, Mr. MacKaye is lacking. His gift has not yet proved itself essentially dramatic. I use the word advisedly. For the external arts of the theatre he has, as becomes a son of Steele MacKaye, an unfailing instinct. His dialogue [in *Jeanne d'Arc*] is firm and natural. He never fails to visualize, and externally to vitalize, his scenes. His pictorial projection of Jeanne's visions shows an expert hand in what the profession calls effects. He probably could not if he would write an unactable part. But he has never yet evinced the clear intellect and firm grasp of the conflicts of character and impulse which are essential to the construction of a dynamic stage story. . . .

Mr. MacKaye has, however, as it seems to me, taken an honorable position among modern poetic dramatists. His play has little of the brilliancy of Rostand, little of the dramatic movement and suspense of Stephen Phillips at his best. But it has a quality of its own, which, to me at least, is no less momentous — an unfailing grace of the affections and a sustaining spiritual power. This is the work of a young man finely and characteristically American, who sees life sweetly, with tenderness, depth, and humor, and sees it whole. It is already evident, too, that his talent is as varied as it is fine. *The Canterbury Pilgrims,* published but as yet unacted, is a brisk and ebullient comedy of Chaucer, and *The Wife of Bath* full of the childlike gayety and childlike poetry of old England. *The Scarecrow,* neither published nor acted, is a keen and striking satirical phantasy of puritan New England, founded on Hawthorne's *Feathertop.* As yet [he is] in his early thirties; the success of *Jeanne d'Arc,* which is extraordinary, should prove the means of broadening Mr. MacKaye's talent and giving it scope. The task of creating a poetic drama in the twentieth century is not without difficulties of the gravest; but there is abundant indication that it lies within his powers.

arthur hobson quinn

EUGENE O'NEILL

It is just that quality of imagination, of the ability to see more in a character or a situation than someone else, and to express that vision with skill and sincerity, which makes the work of Mr. Eugene O'Neill so important. He takes his material where he finds it — in New York City, in a New England village, on an island in the Atlantic Ocean, or in a sanitarium for tuberculosis. He is not concerned with preaching any doctrine or advocating any cause. Like all other great dramatists, he is interested in human character, and he places that character in an imagined situation and allows it to work out its own salvation or ruin. He is not concerned whether the ending be happy or unhappy in the usual sense; he is determined, however, that it be logical. He is not bound by any theories of dramatic art but he feels himself at liberty to try new modes of expression if he can secure better effects by so doing. But he never tries new methods simply because they are new; he knows the distinction between originality and mere difference.

Like all writers of importance, Mr. O'Neill is constantly misunderstood. To those who have seen and read his plays and have been privileged to have his own interpretation of them, there is no possibility of misunderstanding. He is too great a dramatist to be classified or to be placed in a school of playwrights. He, like Napoleon, is himself an ancestor. But it is true that to a certain degree he is of his own age and place. His work, considered as a whole, has an underlying philosophy, the expression of deep sympathy with the individual who is oppressed or misunderstood and who is matching his strength against opposing forces that threaten to crush him. In this sense he is akin to the other playwrights of whom we have spoken. But he differs from them also in many ways. His characters are more strongly conceived and more sharply drawn. His plays are framed with a keener sense of the theater, in which he grew up, and he has the ability to modify his method to suit his material.

In *Beyond the Horizon*, his first long play, he drew the character of a dreamer, Robert Mayo, the son of a farmer, who hates the narrow

From "The American Spirit in Comedy and Tragedy" in *The English Journal*, XIII (January, 1924), 1–10. Reprinted with the permission of the National Council of Teachers of English and Arthur H. Quinn, Jr.

life of the farm and is about to realize his dream of a voyage to far-off places which are to him the romance his life has always craved. He gives them up at the call of a woman's passion and ruin comes in consequence. But because he has had the dreams, he feels at the end that the struggle was worth while. It is a pity that *Beyond the Horizon* was not played as it was written. In the stage version the last scene was omitted and the great message of hope was not given. There is hope, too, in the last scene of *The Straw* although the shadow of death hovers over it. Here the stage performance brought out qualities that were not so apparent in reading, and it will be long before I shall forget the appeal of Mr. Otto Kruger as Stephen Murray for the right to hope that his newfound love shall save Eileen Carmody, even at the gates of death. Notwithstanding this remarkable acting quality, *The Straw* was not a popular success. *Anna Christie,* however, has met with great favor, both here and abroad, and while it has not the spiritual quality of *Beyond the Horizon*, it is even better constructed from the dramatic point of view. It contains three remarkable characters, not a bit overdrawn, yet theatrically effective. Old Chris Christopherson is a sailor who attributes all the ill success of his life to "that old davil-sea," and this obsession of his runs through the play like the *motif* of an opera. Anna Christie, his daughter, has been sent by him to an inland country home to save her from this evil influence but has been led astray by one of her boy-cousins and has sunk lower until she has become the inmate of a house of illfame. In the first act, after Chris has painted a glowing picture of her to his tavern associates, she presents herself in a scene which the acting of Miss Pauline Lord made superb. In the second act there is a wonderful picture of the cleansing effect which the sea and the fog are having upon her nature; and then the third character, Matt Burke, the gigantic Irish sailor, rises up out of the sea and makes love to her. The climax of the play comes when she reveals her past to her lover and her father. There is no sentimentalizing of the situation, and she dominates it through the supreme right of her suffering. Mr. O'Neill has been accused of truckling to popular approval in bringing about her lover's return after he had at first left her. But there is no "happy ending" in *Anna Christie,* for the marriage may be only the beginning of another tragedy.

In two of his plays Mr. O'Neill departed from the customary dramatic form with striking success. *The Emperor Jones* is laid in an island in the West Indies, "not yet self-determined by white marines," and is a study of the effect of terror upon a negro from the United States who has dominated the natives by the force of his personality, but whose reign has come to an end. After a remarkable scene in which these facts are brought out through his conversation with a British trader, the remaining seven scenes are concerned with his flight through the forest and his capture and death at the hands of the rebels. In six of these scenes no one speaks but "the emperor," and Mr. O'Neill violates cheerfully and successfully the rule that monologue must not be permitted on the stage. Monologue is supposed to lead to monotony, but in *The Emperor Jones* variety is secured by the steady increase in the intensity of the shades of terror. The play must be read, and better, seen, to appreciate the force of this appeal as the negro is led back in his visions through his prenatal and preracial life. And the most important fact remains that though we may not like the man we cannot help admiring his pluck, and we agree with the British trader as the latter looks at him lying dead: "Gawd blimey, but yer died in the 'eighth o' style, anyhow!"

In *The Hairy Ape* Mr. O'Neill continued to express his dramatic idea in the form of scenes without division into acts, thereby securing an acceleration of power. In this play, his hero, a stoker on an ocean liner, is the representative of physical force, which, if it remains unguided, may do great harm, but which carries the world on. The "Yank," as he is called, has no resentment at first against those who idle while he is working. He "belongs" — they do not, that is all. But when the daughter of the owner of the line of steamers comes down to the stokehole to see the animals at work, and he sees the horror in her face when she looks at him, he determines to be revenged upon her and her kind for the insult. The futility of his attempt makes up the rest of the play, and again, as in *The Emperor Jones*, while we dislike the "Yank" for his brutality, we cannot but recognize the effort toward something higher which was as the bottom even of his revenge.

The tragedies of Eugene O'Neill, with the exception of *Diff'rent*, meet the highest test — that they shall leave us spiritually exalted. Even if the struggle of the individual against fate or circumstances is a failure, that effort has been worth while, and the hero or heroine secures our sympathy. This, after all, is the great test of the value of a play. . . .

walter j. meserve

SIDNEY HOWARD AND THE
SOCIAL DRAMA OF THE TWENTIES

Underlying a great portion of the American plays written after the turn of the twentieth century there is a social consciousness and a concern for realism that distinguish trends in American drama. At their beginning they formed dual and almost parallel movements, the most significant in late 19th century American drama: the development of a social comedy, and the Rise of Realism in the drama. Numerous plays began to caricature aspects of society and also to reflect the literary interest in realism. Later, after the shock resulting from the American production of Ibsen's *Ghosts* in 1889, Ibsenism lent a certain unifying force to these trends. But it was not until the 1920's that social drama became a serious and dominant trend, part of a national growth in American drama which was reflected in the plays of Maxwell Anderson, Philip Barry, Paul Green, Rachel Crothers, Eugene O'Neill, S. N. Behrman, Elmer Rice, and Sidney Howard. Of these dramatists, only Sidney Howard produced his most significant plays during the twenties. During this decade which is now remembered mainly for the work of the Provincetown Players and the plays of Eugene O'Neill, Sidney Howard emerged as the first major writer of social drama in a long line of development that leads from James A. Herne to Tennessee Williams.

Writing a preface to *Lucky Sam McCarver*, Howard admitted that as a thinker he was neither profound nor original. In an age which makes every man his own "puffer" such modesty and honesty is refreshing in any writer, and one is perhaps tempted to be overly charitable in the face of such self-depreciation.

But after some thought one must conclude that Sidney Howard was right. This does not mean, of course, that he was superficial or that he was a poor dramatist, but rather that his plays do not lend themselves to searching literary criticism. Generally, his plays do not emphasize intellectual depth or imaginative development, but they do suggest a potent new force for a movement in American drama. To this trend he added an artistic mastery which deserves a certain critical acclaim.

The social drama of the twenties seems to have developed from

Modern Drama, VI (December, 1963), 256–266. Reprinted by permission of A. C. Edwards, editor of *Modern Drama*.

several existing categories of early twentieth century drama, fused by the term *social* but vaguely distinguished as social comedy, social realism, and social melodrama — all of which showed the influence of Ibsenism. In 1890 Alfred Hennequin in "Characteristics of American Drama" (*Arena*, I [May, 1890], 700–709) maintained that French melodrama and English melodrama had combined to produce a new type of American play — the social melodrama. That such a social drama was not popular at this time, however, is made clear by the frightened and frigid reception given James A. Herne's *Margaret Fleming* and by declarations like Daniel Frohman's in "The Tendencies of the American Stage" (*Cosmopolitan*, XXXVIII [November, 1904], 15–22) that American audiences looked for "vivacity and rapid sequence" in plays rather than the "food for thought" which the French and Germans preferred. Seven years after this comment, Clayton Hamilton, writing on "Melodrama, Old and New" (*Bookman*, XXXIII [May, 1911], 309–14), re-emphasized the same idea as he moaned the changes in modern melodrama. In the past he had enjoyed the melodrama of Augustin Daly, David Belasco, and Owen Davis — all vivid and violent, sweet and sentimental. Now Hamilton found "a new species of melodrama that is ashamed of itself" as it takes the form of "a serious study of contemporary social problems."

With this fusion of comedy, realism, and melodrama, touched lightly by Ibsenism, social drama was being born in America. It was a slow process, but by the first decade of the twentieth century, attitudes and issues had become accepted materials for plays — social, political, economic, religious, or moral. Among the numerous writers of what must be called realistic social melodrama before World War I, one of the most successful was Eugene Walter whose drama, *The Easiest Way*, 1908, was a striking portrayal of a woman who was unable to overcome her own basic weakness and the temptations of society. *Fine Feathers*, 1913, another Walter play, dramatized with some effect the evils of greed and temptation in the modern world. The only playwrights of this period, in fact, whose names are likely to be recalled, wrote seriously of social problems: William Vaughn Moody, *The Great Divide*, 1909; Edward Sheldon, *The Boss*, 1916; Charles Rann Kennedy, and Rachel Crothers. Kennedy's *The Servant in the House*, 1908, might be called a social gospel play, a denunciation of weak and ineffective Christianity; while *The Idol Breakers*, 1914, a much underrated play, quite profoundly dramatized in symbolic fantasy the struggle of the idealist to obtain that freedom which is both truth and beauty. Starting with *He and She* in 1911 and continuing for the next twenty odd years, Miss Crothers concerned herself with the social problems of her day and almost every year contributed a play of some pleasure and value to American theater.

In a theater where profundity was not a common ingredient of drama, Eugene Walter, Charles Rann Kennedy, Jesse Lynch Williams, Owen Davis, and Rachel Crothers infused into their plays both serious thought and some skill in handling the problems of dramaturgy.

Into this stream of American drama, Sidney Howard launched his plays and by so doing, added an imagination and talent, which, guided by a new sense of realism, gave social drama a new dignity and position in the eyes of the audiences and critics, both in America and abroad. The 1920's were his years of major achievement, and his most worthy plays of the decade were *They Knew What They Wanted, Lucky Sam McCarver, Ned McCobb's Daughter,* and *The Silver Cord.* Later plays of the 1930's, *The Late Christopher Bean, Alien Corn,* and *The Ghost of Yankee Doodle,* showed his continued interest in his main theme but also suggested a decline in dramatic power. Yet Charles Whitman in his 1936 edition of *Representative Modern Dramas* could call Sidney Howard "one of the most accomplished of living American playwrights." And Joseph Wood Krutch in *American Drama Since 1918* could write that "Mr. Howard's plays are among the best ever written in America."

Although one finds Sidney Howard's plays of major significance in the development of modern social drama in America and his themes still vital and meaningful, candor forces one to agree with Mr. Krutch on only two Howard plays. In spite of obvious defects, *They Knew What They Wanted* is an epoch-marking play for its sense of humanity and its insights into social morality. Statements by Howard and current critics notwithstanding, however, it is a modern version of the Paolo-Francesca love story of Wagner's *Tristan and Isolde* only in a very vague fashion. No characters in the ancient or modern stories bear close comparison, and the plots have only a vague resemblance at one or two points. The conflict in Howard's play, in fact, is completely different from that of the tragic lovers whom Dante celebrates. One might more advantageously compare the play with James A. Herne's *Margaret Fleming.* Margaret and Phillip Fleming no less than Tony and Amy, know what they want, and have either the strength to arrange it (as Tony and Margaret do) or the weakness to accept it (as Amy and Phillip). Although parts of *They Knew What They Wanted* are talky and even irrelevant to the main action of the play, in Tony, Howard created his most successful character. Most appealing, most real, most expedient among Howard's people, Tony is also the one most able to deal with the exigencies of the world. After struggling with his pride, Tony makes a discovery, acts upon it in both a socially expedient and Christian manner, and becomes not the most miserable of men but a "most happy fella."

For different reasons *The Silver Cord* must be judged one of the best social-thesis dramas written in America, although it, too, suffers from some preachment. In this play Howard dramatizes the professional mother, Mrs. Phelps, who fights to possess her two sons: she successfully destroys the love of Robert and his fiancée, Hester, but fails to break up the marriage of her older son, David, and Christina, a woman as determined as herself. Rejecting the traditional romantic thesis of filial obligation, Howard presented an individuality which becomes a major thesis in most of his plays. "An embryological accident," says Christina, "is no ground for honour." Actually, the Freudian overtones and Oedipus complex which explain this leftover romanticism of the 18th century heroic tragedy are devices for manipulation rather than motivation. They add, however, a unifying modern touch which also determines the melodramatic-comedy level of the work by giving the audience an opportunity to explain, to hate, and therefore to feel superior to the characters in the play.

The real basis of the play as it becomes a serious study of a social problem, however, is not Hester's romantic comment on children — "Have 'em. Love 'em. And then leave 'em be." — but a distinction between "life and self." Christina pretends to understand this doctrine as she tells about her professor in medical school, "the great god Krause," who could write about his approaching death and then go off sledding. But only Krause has the secret. Only a god can make the proper distinction, Howard seems to be saying. Although the biologist Christina is obviously an apostle of "life" in Howard's mind, the play becomes largely the dramatization of a conflict between a professional mother and an independent and ambitious wife. Both deserve some sympathy, yet each struggles desperately for the fulfillment of "self." Christina, however, is not morally disfigured as Mrs. Phelps is. Her selfish concern for her career is balanced by her more healthy attitude toward the life of her unborn child and the freedom of life which she knows that she and Dave, her husband, must have to be happy.

The conflict is dramatized with great effect in this play, and Mrs. Phelps is singularly diabolical in ways that invite comparison with Laura in Strindberg's *The Father*. The play is marred, however, by the weakness of the Freudian faulted Phelps boys, Howard's impulses for moral preachment, the lack of any real dramatic discovery on Christina's part, and the very late and unmotivated decision by Dave. Obviously the thesis of the play, "life and self," is most difficult to dramatize because in the play "self" must be centered in one person and "life" in another. At the end of the play the audience may be happy because "life" has triumphed over "self:" Christina has defeated the villainess, helped free the innocent girl, and gained her personal objective in the bargain. But Christina is not herself free from the demands of "self," and Dave may very well be stepping from one trap into another. As a social drama with a Freudian thesis, however — the level on which the play was most generally understood — it was successful and showed dramatic power on the stage.

During the twenties Howard adapted seven plays and wrote seven more of which only four seem worth analysis. Next in significance to *They Knew What They Wanted* and *The Silver Cord* are *Lucky Sam McCarver* and *Ned McCobb's Daughter* — one a theater failure and the other a success but both examples of the social drama in which Howard excelled. Each is concerned with a strong character in a series of situations contrived to dramatize those personal qualities which react powerfully to social conditions and frustrations. *Lucky Sam McCarver* starts out as an analysis of Sam McCarver but is more effective as the story of a woman who desperately wants love from a man who has only money to give. Unlike *Ned McCobb's Daughter*, it is an unhappy social drama of irresponsible people: a frustrated woman and a materialistic man who will always be, as one person tells him, "disappointed in the universe." Social conditions provide the background for Ned McCobb's daughter, Carrie, to show the superiority of her character and her Yankee determination to get what she wants. Mainly Howard's characters know what they want, but Howard invariably controlled their destinies. Although he frequently tempered his moral judgments with real mercy, within his definitions of right and wrong he was completely conventional in meting out rewards and punishments.

It was perhaps inevitable that Sidney Howard should write social drama. Man's social problems interested him before he became a playwright, although his services in World War I, first as an ambulance driver and then as an aviator concerned with destroying life, perhaps reflect some confusion as to how he would satisfy his idealism. After the war he became a radical reporter for the *New Republic* before joining the editorial staff of the old *Life* and later working as a feature writer for Hearst's *International Magazine*. His personal idealism as a crusader, therefore, may explain Joe's polemic on individual rights in *They Knew What They Wanted*, the Keystone Cops Federal men in *Ned McCobb's Daughter*, and the bitter attitudes toward war in *The Ghost of Yankee Doodle*. Certainly his independence of spirit may be traced in the theme of individual freedom which permeates his plays.

This independence of spirit, however, did not extend to the form in which he wrote his plays. He was not an experimenter at a time when many were experimenting. It is commonplace, of course, to call him a traditionalist, but his attitude toward the dignity of the dramatist seems to carry him beyond this position. For him the dramatist was only a "vicarious actor" who depended upon the actor to make his work meaningful. "The best that any dramatist can hope," he stated, "is that his play may prove to be a worthy vehicle." With this attitude he followed the theories of Augustin Daly and Daniel Frohman, and the "Laws of Dramatic Construction" put forth in 1886 by Bronson Howard who disregarded literary value and thought of a play only as stage production. As a result both Howards emphasized, among other things, the "satisfactory" ending of a play — that which would satisfy the audience whether or not it revealed true character. Sidney Howard, however, was never able to leave his play completely in the hands of the actors. His technique suggests, perhaps unconsciously, the inadequacy of some of his lines as well as his distrust of actors or readers to interpret his ideas correctly. One immediately recalls his innumerable and sometimes insufferably clever stage directions. When reprimanding Tony in *They Knew What They Wanted*, Father McKee becomes a "very severe shepherd." Mrs. Phelps' "wee mousie" activities indicate the part that stage directions play in *The Silver Cord*. Clearly some of his stage directions were a vain attempt to be witty and/or "literary" in the most common sense of the term. Too often, however, stage directions in his plays, rather than simply describing movements, indicate a definite interpretation which perhaps only reinforces Howard's position as a "vicarious actor."

Generally Howard followed the realistic patterns established by his American predecessors, but he cannot be denied the courage — and the success — with which he brought new points of view to the theater and strengthened some of the old. With the strong realistic social morality of *They Knew What They Wanted* he followed the trend of the past but revolted from it in the same way that Sinclair Lewis made use of the realism of William Dean Howells and yet rebelled from its narrowness. In *The Silver Cord* he insinuated a Freudian interpretation with such success that the illustration, at least, remains enduring in the history of American drama. Carrie McCobb is, of course, not an innovation but another realistic Yankee character, who ranks above James A. Herne's Uncle Nat Berry, memorable Downeaster in *Shore Acres* and Owen Davis's forceful Yankee girl, Jane, in his Pulitzer Prize winner, *Icebound*.

As a craftsman of the theater Howard found his greatest success in creating social drama from a mixture of realism, melodrama, and comedy. His major interest in his plays, however, was the people, as the titles of his plays indicate. Psychological interpretation of character becomes a part of his two best plays. More exuberant than thoughtful, however, he was frequently satisfied to have his characters simply react emotionally to strong stimuli. In *They Knew What They Wanted*, for example, Tony controls his passion, rises above his pride, and in strength rather than in weakness rationalizes the situation which confronts him: "What you have done is mistake in da head, not in da heart"; he says, "Mistake in head is no matter." Howard himself showed in his characters that he agreed with this idea: emotion is more important than intellect — and certainly easier to dramatize. A biologist with a Ph.D., Christina in *The Silver Cord* at first tries to resolve her difficulties with Mrs. Phelps through reason, but her attempts fail; intellect is not enough. Even after she tries to combine intellect and emotion, she does not become a completely satisfying heroine because her argument is cooled by the force of intelligence rather than heated by emotional conviction. Howard forgot one of his basic rules in this play. Consequently, the audience cannot accept without question the positive victory of "life" which Howard obviously indicates in his conclusion.

Carrie, Ned McCobb's daughter, has strong Yankee convictions which control much of the action of the play. Babe, her brother-in-law, tells her: "You got a wonnerful character, Carrie. . . . An' dat's what counts in dis world. . . . Beauty fades but character goes on forever." He admires the strength which Carries possesses, and he thinks her smart. Before the end of the play she shows that she is shrewd enough to defeat his game, but her motivation is clearly from the heart rather than the head. One of Howard's few plays with a sad ending is *Lucky Sam McCarver*. Sam is a hardened materialist who frankly uses his wife and her name and sees nothing beyond his growing empire. Having lost human compassion, lost the ability to feel, he can only think and contrive; in this condition he has no value in Howard's world which is essentially a world of action and feeling rather than thought.

In large part Howard dramatizes emotions in his plays through expertly contrived scenes of fast moving action and by rapid emotional changes in his characters. The festive scene in *They Knew What They Wanted*, the scene in Venice in Act III of *Lucky Sam McCarver*, the final scene of *Ned McCobb's Daughter* which climaxes the melodramatic cops and robbers plot, or a number of scenes from *The Silver Cord* — all suggest Howard's concern for strong emotional scenes of theatrical effectiveness in which his characters react strongly to one another. Violence is also a part of the life he portrays: the shooting of Monty Garside and the contrived death of Carlotta in *Lucky Sam McCarver*, the death of Captain McCobb and the activities of the Federal Men in *Ned McCobb's Daughter*, the use of the shotgun in *They Knew What They Wanted*, the scene in *The Silver Cord* in which Mrs. Phelps tears out the telephone wire. (The placement of the scenes in the last two plays is a tribute to Howard's ability to build successfully the right dramatic effect.) Although emotional changes in characters can be perfectly natural, on some occasions Howard's dramatic effect is marred by the too rapid emotional changes which his characters exercise. In *Ned McCobb's Daughter*, Act III, Carrie changes so abruptly from hysteria to calm certainty and from innocence to cunning that her motivation seems questionable. Mrs. Phelps in *The Silver Cord* also runs the gamut of emotional experiences, quickly changing from one emotion to another in ways that suggest less her neuroticism than Howard's interest in a particular effect.

Of major significance in Howard's success as a dramatist is his use of dramatic irony of situation. Mrs. Phelps' picture of herself as a completely unselfish mother is an ironic contrast to the thesis of the play. *The Silver Cord* is, in fact, a mass of ironies. It is ironic, for example, that the one who has the most normal and healthy point of view in the play, Hester, is supposed to be recovering from a mental breakdown. The ending of the play conveys a masterful double irony when Mrs. Phelps is left with Robert whom earlier in the act she has been led to claim once more as her son in opposition to David who takes "after his father." Finally, and yet unconsciously, she has been forced to tell the truth. There is an ironic turning of tables at the end of *Ned McCobb's Daughter,* but because the play is basically melodramatic any subtlety of technique is missing. *Lucky Sam McCarver* — the very title is ironic — also is built around a basic irony inherent in characters who discover that they have not seen themselves and the world in a realistic perspective. The basic tragi-comic situation in *They Knew What They Wanted* is itself ironic, and it also provides opportunity for irony, such as Tony's fatherly advice that Joe marry a wife like Amy. If Howard has a significant claim to being literary, it is in his use of irony both in character development and situation.

Although secondary to a concern for character and action, Howard's ideas are traceable in his plays and suggest an ideological rationale. Consistent with the general philosophy of the twenties, an underlying theme in Eugene O'Neill's work, and Howard's social radicalism, there is inherent in all his plays an ideal of individual freedom, the independence of self. Nearly seventy-five years before, a Mrs. Sidney Bateman had dramatized the idea that everything was moved by "that great motive power — self!" (*Self,* 1857) Howard plucked the same string but in a different rhythm. Whereas O'Neill searched for an understanding of self throughout his plays, Howard assumed a knowledge and an identification, and on a social rather than a philosophical level dramatized the attempted romantic escape of the self from all that was confining. Howard's treatment of this romantic escape may be seen in two groups of people he dramatized: those who distinguish between "life and self," and those who do not. Essentially, the second group seeks freedom and selfish irresponsibility, while the first wants freedom with responsibility. The second group Howard punished by trapping them in their own selfishness; the first he rewarded with freedom and potential happiness.

Dissatisfied, frustrated, frightened, or lonely, Howard's characters are motivated by self in their desperate struggles to escape to freedom. Lucky Sam McCarver is driven by a selfish desire for material success: yet he is also trying to escape something. He is "disappointed in the universe." "Every year ashamed of what last year was!" his wife, Carlotta tells him; "Wiping the slate clean! And what for? What for?" At the end of the play, with Carlotta dead, he walks away with a certain freedom — although never to be satisfied — but with never a doubt, Howard writes, as to "his own self-sufficient power and destiny." Self is clearly the motivating force in *The Silver Cord*. Mrs. Phelps is diabolically hypocritical in disclaiming a "selfish hair" in her head, but Christina also refuses to sacrifice her career by allowing David to stay near his mother and build Mrs. Phelps' manor. Christina is trying to escape the almost overwhelming power of Mrs. Phelps who desperately fears the loneliness that her future forebodes. The past has been her life, and, symbolized by David's bedroom, she confesses to having "made a little shrine of it." Both women assert "self" to escape domination by the other. Yet to achieve happiness one cannot be limited by self; one must have broader horizons, strive to be god-like; one must distinguish between life and self. Both Lucky Sam McCarver and Mrs. Phelps are trapped by their own selfishness and doomed, just as Doc Haggett is trapped in *The Late Christopher Bean.*

In Howard's other major plays his characters are motivated by "self" to escape certain undesirable aspects of life, and yet each is aware of life beyond self and the responsibility which freedom demands. Both Amy and Tony in *They Knew What They Wanted* assert "self" to escape their individual loneliness. They know what they want, however, and in the face of difficulty each can sacrifice the pride of self and achieve the happiness and freedom that comes with the larger perspective of life. Christina, from *The Silver Cord,* makes the same distinctions, at least in Howard's view, and is justly rewarded. Although *Ned McCobb's Daughter* is too superficial a melodrama to permit great sensitivity in characters, Howard's technique is clear. All action centers upon the single character, Carrie, who is designated as "responsible" early in the play when she says that raising kids is the "only thing on earth worth makin' a fuss over!" To build the addition to her Spa — which is her major objective in the play — she overcomes all difficulties. Self is satisfied; her individual freedom is assured; and there is that vague nobility which melodrama assures. A later and better play, *Alien Corn,* shows a romantic escape to individual freedom, motivated by self, yet balanced by a sense of superiority and an awareness of the distinction between life and self.

A dominant idea in Howard's plays is presented in the title of his first popular success: *They Knew What They Wanted.* With this idea he reflects the distinctive and positive individualism of the social drama of the 1920's and also distinguishes this social drama from what came before and what eventually followed. Social drama and melodrama before and during World War I generally emphasized the force of social conventions. Before *Nice People* in 1920 and *Expressing Willie* in 1924 Rachel Crothers did not allow her characters to assert themselves beyond social acceptability. Nor did Jesse Lynch Williams' *Why Marry?* suggest anything more than the acceptance of social custom. With very few exceptions playwrights dramatized the subjection of the individual to the conventions of society. During the 1930's the tone of American social drama again changed, although the individualism of the twenties did not completely die out. A strong trend in the thirties, however, dramatized man as representative of a social class and frequently victimized by the social structures.

Although characters in American social drama of the 1920's generally knew what they wanted, not all were successful in achieving their desire. For example, S. N. Behrman's hero, Clark Storey, in *The Second Man*, 1927, knew what he wanted and kept it. So did Mary and Jim Hutton in Philip Barry's *Paris Bound*, 1927, as well as Lissa in his earlier play *In a Garden*, 1924. Maxwell Anderson's *Saturday's Children*, 1927, discover what they want and try, although in a very romantic fashion, to get it. Earlier, 1923, Jane in Davis's *Icebound* was successful in getting what she wanted. On the other hand, Paul Green's Abraham McCrannie from *In Abraham's Bosom*, 1926, knew exactly what he wanted but couldn't gain it. Even the characters in Elmer Rice's *The Adding Machine*, 1923, and Sophie Treadwell's *Machinal* fit into this thesis. Exceptions can be found, of course, but Howard should be credited with putting his finger upon an idea which helps define the social drama of the 1920's.

During a decade in which the achievement of one dramatist overshadowed the work of all others, Sidney Howard escapes notice as the first major writer of social drama in modern American drama. Although he generally followed an established trend in American drama, Howard, in his best plays, brought an artistic mastery to the creation of his characters, a social perspective which made his plays transcend the limitations of a contemporary social drama, and an attitude toward life which helped characterize the social drama of the twenties.

EUGENE O'NEILL

Whatever is unclear about Eugene O'Neill, one thing is certainly clear — his genius. We do not like the word nowadays, feeling that it is one of the blurb words of criticism. We demand that literature be a guide to life, and when we do that we put genius into a second place, for genius assures us of nothing but itself. Yet when we stress the action-able conclusions of an artist's work, we are too likely to forget the power of genius itself, quite apart from its conclusions. The spectacle of the human mind in action is vivifying; the explorer need discover nothing so long as he has adventured. Energy, scope, courage — these may be admirable in themselves. And in the end these are often what endure best. The ideas expressed by works of the imagination may be built into the social fabric and taken for granted; or they may be rejected; or they may be outgrown. But the force of their utterance comes to us over millennia. We do not read Sophocles or Aeschylus for the right answer; we read them for the force with which they represent life and attack its moral complexity. In O'Neill, despite the many failures of his art and thought, this force is inescapable.

But a writer's contemporary audience is inevitably more interested in the truth of his content than in the force of its expression; and O'Neill himself has always been ready to declare his own ideological preoccu-pation. His early admirers — and their lack of seriousness is a reproach to American criticism — were inclined to insist that O'Neill's content was unimportant as compared to his purely literary interest and that he injured his art when he tried to think. But the appearance of *Days Without End* has made perfectly clear the existence of an organic and progressive unity of thought in all O'Neill's work and has brought it into the critical range of the two groups whose own thought is most sharply formulated, the Catholic and the Communist. Both discovered what O'Neill had frequently announced, the religious nature of all his effort.

Not only has O'Neill tried to encompass more of life than most American writers of his time but, almost alone among them, he has persistently tried to *solve* it. When we understand this we understand

The New Republic, LXXXVIII (September 23, 1936), 176–179. Reprinted by permission of *The New Republic* and Mr. Lionel Trilling.

that his stage devices are no fortuitous technique; his masks and abstractions, his double personalities, his drum beats and engine rhythms are the integral and necessary expression of his temper of mind and the task it set itself. Realism is uncongenial to that mind and that task and it is not in realistic plays like *Anna Christie* and *The Straw* but rather in such plays as *The Hairy Ape, Lazarus Laughs* and *The Great God Brown*, where he is explaining the world in parable, symbol and myth, that O'Neill is most creative. Not the minutiae of life, not its feel and color and smell, not its nuance and humor, but its "great inscrutable forces" are his interest. He is always moving toward the finality which philosophy sometimes, and religion always, promises. Life and death, good and evil, spirit and flesh, male and female, the all and the one, Anthony and Dionysius — O'Neill's is a world of these antithetical absolutes such as religion rather than philosophy conceives, a world of pluses and minuses; and his literary effort is an algebraic attempt to solve the equations.

In one of O'Neill's earliest one-act plays, the now unprocurable *Fog*, a Poet, a Business Man and a Woman with a Dead Child, shipwrecked and adrift in an open boat, have made fast to an iceberg. When they hear the whistle of a steamer, the Business Man's impulse is to call for help, but the Poet prevents him lest the steamer be wrecked on the fog-hidden berg. But a searching party picks up the castaways and the rescuers explain that they had been guided to the spot by a child's cries; the Child, however, has been dead a whole day. This little play is a crude sketch of the moral world that O'Neill is to exploit. He is to give an ever increasing importance to the mystical implications of the Dead Child, but his earliest concern is with the struggle between the Poet and the Business Man.

It is, of course, a struggle as old as morality, especially interesting to Europe all through its industrial nineteenth century, and it was now engaging America in the second decade of its twentieth. A conscious artistic movement had raised its head to declare irreconcilable strife between the creative and the possessive ideal. O'Neill was an integral part — indeed, he became the very symbol — of that Provincetown group which represented the growing rebellion of the American intellectual against a business civilization. In 1914 his revolt was simple and socialistic; in a poem in The Call he urged the workers of the world not to fight, asking them if they wished to "bleed and groan — for Guggenheim" and "give your lives — for Standard Oil." By 1917 his feelings against business had become symbolized and personal. "My soul is a submarine," he said in a poem in The Masses:

My aspirations are torpedoes.
I will hide unseen
Beneath the surface of life
Watching for ships,
Dull, heavy-laden merchant ships,
Rust-eaten, grimy galleons of commerce
Wallowing with obese assurance,
Too sluggish to fear or wonder,
Mocked by the laughter of the waves
And the spit of disdainful spray.

I will destroy them
Because the sea is beautiful.

The ships against which O'Neill directed his torpedoes were the cultural keels laid in the yards of American business and their hulls were first to be torn by artistic realism. Although we now see the often gross sentimentality of the "S.S. Glencairn" plays and remember with O'Neill's own misgiving the vaudeville success of *In the Zone,* we cannot forget that, at the time, the showing of a forecastle on the American stage was indeed something of a torpedo. Not, it is true, into the sides of Guggenheim and Standard Oil, but of the little people who wallowed complacently in their wake.

But O'Neill, not content with staggering middle-class complacency by a representation of how the other half lives, undertook to scrutinize the moral life of the middle class and dramatized the actual struggle between Poet and Business Man. In his first long play, *Beyond the Horizon,* the dreamer destroys his life by sacrificing his dream to domesticity; and the practical creator, the farmer, destroys his by turning from wheat-raising to wheat-gambling. It is a conflict O'Neill is to exploit again and again. Sometimes, as in *Ile* or *Gold,* the lust for gain transcends itself and becomes almost a creative ideal, but always its sordid origin makes it destructive. To O'Neill the acquisitive man, kindly and insensitive, practical and immature, became a danger to life and one that he never left off attacking.

But it developed, strangely, that the American middle class had no strong objection to being attacked and torpedoed; it seemed willing to be sunk for the insurance that was paid in a new strange coin. The middle class found that it consisted of two halves, bourgeoisie and booboisie. The booboisie might remain on the ship but the bourgeoisie could, if it would, take refuge on the submarine. Mencken and Nathan, who sponsored the O'Neill torpedoes, never attacked the middle class but only its boobyhood. Boobish and sophisticated: these were the two categories of art; spiritual freedom could be bought at the price of finding "Jurgen" profound. And so, while the booboisie prosecuted

CRITICS: LIONEL TRILLING 21

Desire under the Elms, the bourgeoisie swelled the subscription lists of the Provincetown Playhouse and helped the Washington Square Players to grow into the Theatre Guild. An increasingly respectable audience awarded O'Neill no less than three Pulitzer prizes, the medal of the American Academy of Arts and Sciences and a Yale Doctorate of Letters.

O'Neill did not win his worldly success by the slightest compromise of sincerity. Indeed, his charm consisted in his very integrity and hieratic earnestness. His position changed, not absolutely, but relatively to his audience, which was now the literate middle class caught up with the intellectual middle class. O'Neill was no longer a submarine; he had become a physician of souls. Beneath his iconoclasm his audience sensed reassurance.

The middle class is now in such literary disrepute that a writer's ability to please it is taken as the visible mark of an internal rottenness. But the middle class is people; prick them and they bleed, and whoever speaks sincerely to and for flesh and blood deserves respect. O'Neill's force derives in large part from the force of the moral and psychical upheaval of the middle class; it wanted certain of its taboos broken and O'Neill broke them. He was the Dion Anthony to its William Brown; Brown loved Dion: his love was a way of repenting for his own spiritual clumsiness.

Whoever writes sincerely about the middle class must consider the nature and the danger of the morality of "ideals," those phosphorescent remnants of a dead religion with which the middle class meets the world. This had been Ibsen's great theme, and now O'Neill undertook to investigate for America the destructive power of the ideal — not merely the sordid ideal of the Business Man but even the "idealistic" ideal of the Poet. The Freudian psychology was being discussed and O'Neill dramatized its simpler aspects in *Diff'rent* to show the effects of the repression of life. Let the ideal of chastity repress the vital forces, he was saying, and from this fine girl you will get a filthy harridan. The modern life of false ideals crushes the affirmative and creative nature of man; Pan, forbidden the light and warmth of the sun, grows "sensitive and self-conscious and proud and revengeful" — becomes the sneering Mephistophelean mask of Dion.

The important word is *self-conscious,* for "ideals" are part of the "cheating gestures which constitute the vanity of personality." "Life is all right if you let it alone," says Cybel, the Earth Mother of "The Great God Brown." But the poet of *Welded* cannot let it alone; he and his wife, the stage directions tell us, move in circles of light that represent "auras of egotism" and the high ideals of their marriage are but ways each ego uses to get possession of the other. O'Neill had his answer to this problem of the possessive, discrete personality. Egotism and idealism, he tells us, are twin evils growing from man's suspicion of his life and the remedy is the laughter of Lazarus — "a triumphant, blood-stirring call to that ultimate attainment in which all prepossession with self is lost in an ecstatic affirmation of Life." The ecstatic affirmation of Life, pure and simple, is salvation. In the face of death and pain, man must reply with the answer of Kublai Kaan in *Marco Millions:* "Be proud of life! Know in your heart that the living of life can be noble! Be exalted by life! Be inspired by death! Be humbly proud! Be proudly grateful!"

It may be that the individual life is not noble and that it is full of pain and defeat; it would seem that Eileen Carmody in "The Straw" and Anna Christie are betrayed by life. But no. The "straw" is the knowledge that life is a "hopeless hope" — but still a hope. And nothing matters if you can conceive the whole of life. "Fog, fog, fog all bloody time," is the chord of resolution of *Anna Christie.* "You can't see vhere you vas going, no. Only dat ole davil, sea — she knows." The individual does not know, but life — the sea — knows.

To affirm that life exists and is somehow good — this, then, became O'Neill's quasi-religious poetic function, nor is it difficult to see why the middle class welcomed it. "Brown will still need me," says Dion, "to reassure him he's alive." What to do with life O'Neill cannot say, but there it is. For Ponce de Leon it is the Fountain of Eternity, "the Eternal Becoming which is Beauty." There it is, somehow glorious, somehow meaningless. In the face of despair one remembers that "Always spring comes again bearing life! Always forever again. Spring again! Life again!" To this cycle, even to the personal annihilation in it, the individual must say "Yes." Man inhabits a naturalistic universe and his glory lies in his recognition of its nature and assenting to it; man's soul, no less than the stars and the dust, is part of the Whole and the free man loves the Whole and is willing to be absorbed by it. In short, O'Neill solves the problem of evil by making explicit what men have always found to be the essence of tragedy — the courageous affirmation of life in the face of individual defeat.

But neither a naturalistic view of the universe nor a rapt assent to life constitutes a complete philosophic answer. Naturalism is the noble and realistic attitude that prepares the way for an answer; the tragic affirmation is the emotional crown of a philosophy. Spinoza — with whom O'Neill at this stage of his thought has an obvious affinity — placed between the two an ethic that arranged human values and made the world possible to live in. But O'Neill, faced with a tragic universe, unable to go beyond the febrilely passionate declaration, "Life is," finds the world impossible to live in. The naturalistic universe becomes too heavy a burden for him; its spirituality vanishes; it becomes a universe of cruelly blind matter. "Teach me to be resigned to be an atom," cries Darrell, the frustrated scientist of *Strange Interlude,* and for Nina life is but "a strange dark interlude in the electrical display of God the father" — who is a God deaf, dumb and blind. O'Neill, unable now merely to accept the tragic universe and unable to support it with man's whole strength — his intellect and emotion — prepares to support it with man's weakness: his blind faith.

For the non-Catholic reader O'Neill's explicitly religious solution is likely to be not only insupportable but incomprehensible. Neither St. Francis nor St. Thomas can tell us much about it; it is neither a mystical ecstasy nor the reasoned proof of assumptions. But Pascal can tell us a great deal, for O'Neill's faith, like Pascal's, is a poetic utilitarianism: he needs it and *will* have it. O'Neill rejects naturalism and materialism as Pascal had rejected Descartes and all science. He too is frightened by "the eternal silence of the infinite spaces." Like Pascal, to whom the details of life and the variety and flux of the human mind were repugnant, O'Neill feels that life is empty — having emptied it — and can fill it only by faith in a loving God. The existence of such a God, Pascal knew, cannot be proved save by the heart's need, but this seemed sufficient and he stood ready to stupefy his reason to maintain his faith. O'Neill will do no less. It is perhaps the inevitable way of modern Catholicism in a hostile world.

O'Neill's rejection of materialism involved the familiar pulpit confusion of philosophical materialism with "crass" materialism, that is, with the preference of physical to moral well-being. It is therefore natural that *Dynamo,* the play in which he makes explicit his anti-materialism, should present characters who are mean and little — that, though it contains an Earth Mother, she is not the wise and tragic Cybel but the fat and silly Mrs. Fife, the bovine wife of the atheist dynamo-tender. She, like other characters in the play, allies herself with the Dynamo-God, embodiment both of the materialistic universe and of modern man's sense of his own power. But this new god can only frustrate the forces of life, however much it at first seems life's ally against the Protestant denials, and those who worship it become contemptible and murderous.

And the contempt for humanity which pervades *Dynamo* continues in *Mourning Becomes Electra,* creating, in a sense, the utter hopelessness of that tragedy. Aeschylus had ended his Atreus trilogy on a note of social reconciliation — after the bloody deeds and the awful pursuit of the Furies, society confers its forgiveness, the Furies are tamed to deities of hearth and field: "This day there is a new Order born"; but O'Neill's version has no touch of this resolution. There is no forgiveness in *Mourning Becomes Electra* because, while there is as yet no forgiving

God in O'Neill's cosmos, there is no society either, only a vague chorus of contemptible townspeople. "There's no one left to punish me," says Lavinia. "I've got to punish myself."

It is the ultimate of individual arrogance, the final statement of a universe in which society has no part. For O'Neill, since as far back as *The Hairy Ape*, there has been only the individual and the universe. The social organism has meant nothing. His Mannons, unlike the Atreides, are not monarchs with a relation to the humanity about them, a humanity that can forgive because it can condemn. They act their crimes on the stage of the infinite. The mention of human law bringing them punishment is startlingly incongruous and it is inevitable that O'Neill, looking for a law, should turn to a divine law.

Forgiveness comes in *Ah Wilderness!* the satyr-play that follows the tragedy, and it is significant that O'Neill should have interrupted the composition of *Days Without End* to write it. With the religious answer of the more serious play firm in his mind, with its establishment of the divine law, O'Neill can, for the first time, render the sense and feel of common life, can actually be humorous. Now the family is no longer destructively possessive as he has always represented it, but creatively sympathetic. The revolt of the young son — his devotion to rebels and hedonists, to Shaw, Ibsen and Swinburne — is but the mark of adolescence and in the warm round of forgiving life he will become wisely acquiescent to a world that is not in the least terrible.

But the idyllic life of *Ah, Wilderness!* for all its warmth, is essentially ironical, almost cynical. For it is only when all magnitude has been removed from humanity by the religious answer and placed in the Church and its God that life can be seen as simple and good. The pluses and minuses of man must be made to cancel out as nearly as possible, the equation must be solved to equal nearly zero, before peace may be found. The hero of *Days Without End* has lived for years in a torturing struggle with the rationalistic, questioning "half" of himself which has led him away from piety to atheism, thence to socialism, next to unchastity and finally to the oblique attempt to murder his beloved wife. It is not until he makes an act of submissive faith at the foot of the Cross and thus annihilates the doubting mind, the root of all evil, that he can find peace.

But the annihilation of the questioning mind also annihilates the multitudinous world. *Days Without End,* perhaps O'Neill's weakest play, is cold and bleak; life is banished from it by the vision of the Life Eternal. Its religious content is expressed not so much by the hero's priestly uncle, wise, tolerant, humorous in the familiar literary convention of modern Catholicism, as by the hero's wife, a humorless, puritanical woman who lives on the pietistic-romantic love she bears her husband and on her sordid ideal of his absolute chastity. She is the very embodiment of all the warping, bullying idealism that O'Neill had once attacked. Now, however, he gives credence to this plaster saintliness, for it represents for him the spiritual life of absolutes. Now for the first time he is explicit in his rejection of all merely human bulwarks against the pain and confusion of life — finds in the attack upon capitalism almost an attack upon God, scorns socialism and is disgusted with the weakness of those who are disgusted with social individualism. The peace of the absolute can be bought only at the cost of blindness to the actual.

The philosophic position would seem to be a final one: O'Neill has crept into the dark womb of Mother Church and pulled the universe in with him. Perhaps the very violence of the gesture with which he has taken the position of passivity should remind us of his force and of what such force may yet do even in that static and simple dark. Yet it is scarcely a likely place for O'Neill to remember Dion Anthony's warning: "It isn't enough to be [life's] creature. You've got to create her or she requests you to destroy yourself."

harold clurman

AN INTRODUCTION
TO PLAYS OF THE 1930'S

There is a tendency nowadays to downgrade the thirties. The reason for this is that the prevailing mood of the thirties was what used to be called "left of center." Beginning with the late forties — from the time the phrase about the "iron curtain" became part of the common vocabulary — our "intelligentsia" sounded the retreat. The Roosevelt administration, subjected to sharp criticism not infrequently close to slander, seemed to be in bad odor. "Left of center" might be construed as something worse than liberalism. To be "radical" implied that one might be tainted with some degree of "pink."

Reprinted from *Famous American Plays of the 1930's*. Copyright © 1959 by Harold Clurman and used with the permission of the publishers, Dell Publishing Company, Inc.

A good many of the writers, artists and theatre folk in the thirties were inclined to radicalism. (Had not the Roosevelt administration sponsored the Projects for writers, artists and theatre?) In the early forties the fervor of the thirties was gradually absorbed by the pressures of the war. Since Russia was one of our allies there was less strictly political feeling: everyone was chiefly concerned with victory and the return to peaceful prosperity.

Shortly after the peace conference suspicion of the Soviet Union increased. Radicalism of any sort might be interpreted as "softness" toward the potential enemy. Our artists and writers, including theatre people, had not only shown too much sympathy for social experiment but had also been too emphatic about the real or supposed shortcomings of their own country. At best the enthusiasm of the thirties was now considered a sign of juvenile simple-mindedness, at worst something close to treason.

Around the year 1953 this reaction to the thirties had come close to hysteria. Today there is certainly more calm, but the notion that the thirties was a foolish period persists. Presumably we are now far sounder in our thinking and work than we were then.

There is another aspect to the rather low esteem in which most of the dramatic work of the thirties is now held. The immediate past in the theatre always makes a poor impression. Writing about the twenties, which every student of our theatre history regards as a high point of the American theatre both in volume of activity and in achievement, Joseph Wood Krutch in the early thirties said that the record no longer seemed as bright as it once appeared. Very few of the best plays of that time would endure.

What most of us fail to note in this connection is that very few plays measured in the light of decades or generations have ever "endured." Shakespeare as we know Shakespeare is a nineteenth-century discovery! (He was neglected or disgracefully altered during the seventeenth and eighteenth centuries.) The number of plays which have come down to us from the Greeks of the fifth century B.C. and from the Elizabethan era are a paltry few compared to the number produced. How cavalier was the attitude of our drama critics toward Marlowe's *Tamburlaine* because he was not equal to Shakespeare!

We may explain this paradox through our own theatre-going experience. A play may be both enjoyable and important to us at the moment we see it, but when the circumstances of our lives have changed, it may well have lost its appeal. One of the most popular plays the American theatre has ever produced is the dramatization of *Uncle Tom's Cabin*. No one can deny its importance for its day even if we no longer have much regard for it as literature.

It is downright stupid to sneer at our erstwhile excitement over *Waiting for Lefty* because today a good many people (in Europe at any rate) are waiting for Godot. As theatre-goers we are very rarely able to estimate a play in the present as we shall view it twenty-five years hence. What appeared a very inconsiderable play to England's finest dramatic critic, Bernard Shaw, Oscar Wilde's *The Importance of Being Earnest*, has proved durable beyond anyone's belief when it was first presented.

I recall having seen Robert Sherwood's *The Petrified Forest* (1935) in the company of one of our country's most astute men of letters. He enjoyed it thoroughly. A few days later we spoke on the phone. He remarked that the theatre was a hoax: he had been "taken in" by the play as he watched it, he said, but on further reflection he realized the play's flaws in thought and plot. Most readers who are also playgoers are like that.

We enjoy the "show," but we *think* about the play. There is often a disparity of judgment between the two activities. For though we are intellectually aware that literature and theatre are not identical, we are prone to assume that the text of a play is equivalent to the texture of its production. But a play in the theatre communicates qualities beyond — sometimes, in a bad performance, less than — what we find on the printed page. Thus to evaluate the theatre of any period only with regard to its texts is a falsification.

The plays of the thirties sharpen certain tendencies that were already evident, and comparatively new, in the plays of the twenties. For the twenties, which may be said to represent America's second coming of age in literature (the first might be dated around 1850) and its true coming of age in the theatre, were marked by a rather harsh critical realism. What such men as Frank Norris and Theodore Dreiser had been saying about us in their novels began to be said somewhat more lyrically (though no less vehemently) in the plays of Eugene O'Neill. The theatre is ideologically almost always behind the times because it is a mass medium. It takes a while for people to acknowledge publicly what a few individuals may think and say privately.

It was the artistic pleasure of the twenties to deride, curse, bemoan the havoc, spiritual blindness and absurdity of America's materialistic functionalism with its concomitant acquisitiveness and worship of success.

Another marked feature of the theatrical twenties was the fact that plays which had previously satisfied audiences with the mere tracing of types (or stereotypes) began to strike them as increasingly hollow. Characters began to show their faces on the stage. Psychology was "introduced." Men and women were no longer heroes or villains but "human," a mixture of contradictory traits. The standardized Puritanism typified by the old anti-vice societies became an object of scorn and ridicule.

The sentiment against war in *What Price Glory?* of the twenties was converted into the poignant and pointed satire of Paul Green's *Johnny Johnson* in the thirties. The sense of loneliness which informs O'Neill's pieces is rendered more acute and more general in Steinbeck's *Of Mice and Men* some ten years later. The plight of the colored people in the Heywards' *Porgy* or in Green's *In Abraham's Bosom* is intensified in John Wexley's *They Shall Not Die* in the thirties. The playful probing of Behrman's *The Second Man* in 1927 is given a social connotation in the same author's *Biography* and other of his later plays in the thirties. The laborer as a symbol of inner disharmony within the apparent health of the American commonwealth which we observe in O'Neill's *The Hairy Ape* (1922) becomes a leading theme on a more concrete basis in the thirties.

The most significant difference between the theatre of the twenties and that of the thirties is the emphasis in the later period on the social, economic and political background of the individual psychological case. The Wall Street crash of 1929, the Great Depression of the early thirties with its attendant scar of widespread unemployment, the hopeful attempt to remedy this bitter condition which ensued are the effective causes for the abrupt and drastic change. [*Brief critical comment on representative plays of the thirties follows.*]

Historically speaking [Odets] is the dramatist of the thirties *par excellence*. His immediate sources of inspiration, his point of view, his language, his import and perhaps some of his weaknesses are typical of the thirties.

I am not at all sure that *Awake and Sing!*, first presented by the Group Theatre on February 19, 1935, is the best of Odets' plays. The 1937 *Golden Boy* has a more striking story line and is more varied and personal in its meaning. But *Awake and Sing!* contains the "seed" themes of the Odets plays and indicates most unaffectedly the milieu and the quality of feeling in which his work is rooted. One might even go so far as to say that there is hardly another play of the thirties — except perhaps John Howard Lawson's *Success Story* (1932) — which so directly communicates the very "smell" of New York in the first years of the depression.

The keynotes of the period are struck in *Awake and Sing!* as never again with such warm intimacy. There is first of all the bafflement and all-pervading worry of lower middle-class poverty. This is conveyed in language based on common speech and local New York (including Jewish) idiom, but it is not precisely naturalistic speech, for Odets' writing is a personal creation, essentially lyric, in which vulgarity, tenderness, energy, humor and a headlong idealism are commingled.

What is Odets' basic impulse; what is his "program"? They are contained in Jacob's exhortation to his grandson, "Go out and fight so life shouldn't be printed on dollar bills," and in another reflection, "Life should have some dignity." It seems to me that not only is most of Odets expressed in these bare words but the greater part of the whole cry of the American "progressive" movement — its radicalism if you will — as the artists of the thirties sensed it, is summed up in these innocent mottoes.

The "biblical" fervor in *Awake and Sing!* impels a "revolutionary" conviction expressed in Jacob's comment, "It needs a new world," which leads his grandson to take heart and proclaim, "Fresh blood, arms. We've got 'em. We're glad we're living." This was the "wave" of the thirties. If that wave did not carry us on to the millennium, it is surely the height of folly to believe that it had no vital force and accomplished nothing of value in the arts as well as in our community life.

S. N. Behrman's *End of Summer*, produced by the Theatre Guild on February 17, 1936, gives us the depression period seen from another angle: that of the "privileged" classes. It is a comedy of manners which besides its merits in the way of urbane dialogue, etc., presents a central character who (apart from having a decided semblance to the play's author) is kin to most of the folk who buy the best seats in our metropolitan theatres. Leonie, says Behrman, "is repelled by the gross and the voluptuary: this is not hypocrisy. . . . In the world in which she moves hypocrisy is merely a social lubricant, but this very often springs from a congenital and temperamental inability to face anything but the pleasantest and most immediately appealing and the most flattering aspect of things, in life and in her own nature."

What *End of Summer* presents is the spectacle of such a person confronted by the unhappy phenomenon of mass unemployment, nascent radicalism, spectres of fascism and the ambiguities of the psychoanalysts. The treatment is characteristic of Behrman — joshing, debonair, slightly more lighthearted than the author actually feels.

The lady of the play for the first time meets "the young radicals our colleges are said to be full of nowadays." One such radical, a somewhat fictitious Irish Catholic young fellow, tells the lady, "The world is middle-aged and tired," at which the lady queries, "Can you refresh us?" The young man rejoins, "Refresh you! Leonie, we can rejuvenate you." That was another hope of the youth which during the thirties had reached the ages of twenty-five to thirty-five. It was not altogether a vain hope for, as I have already indicated and shall continue to indicate, there was a young and invigorating spirit that relieved the thirties of its blues and led to concrete benefits.

One of the faults easily spotted in *End of Summer* is also evident in Robert Sherwood's *Idiot's Delight,* produced by the Theatre Guild in the spring of 1936. Just as the young radicals of Behrman's play seem to be known by hearsay rather than by intimate acquaintance, so in *Idiot's Delight* Sherwood's grasp of the European political situation is informed as it were by headlines rather than truly experienced. Thus he makes his French pacifist a Radical-Socialist who speaks of the workers' uprising and alludes to Lenin with reverence, whereas any knowledgeable foreign correspondent could have told Sherwood that the Radical-Socialists of France are the party of small business, abhor Lenin's doctrines and are neither radical nor socialist.

This slight error is worth mentioning because it is symptomatic of a not uncommon failing in American playwrights when they generalize or "intellectualize" on social or ethical themes. It is a species of dilettant-ism which consists of dealing with subjects in which one is certainly interested but not truly familiar.

More cogent than this flaw is the sentiment which inspired Sher-wood to write *Idiot's Delight.* It echoes the American fear of and pro-found estrangement from the facts of European intrigue which led to war. One merit of Sherwood's play is that it gives us an inkling of the moral climate in our country shortly after the Italian-Ethiopian confla-gration and at the outset of the Spanish civil conflict — two omens of the future scarcely understood by an average citizen. Sherwood's "solution" to the problem in his play is the idealistic injunction "You can refuse to fight."

This is significant because it shows that the attitude of our drama-tists, generally speaking, was fundamentally moral rather than, as some are now inclined to believe, political. This explains why Sherwood, whose *Idiot's Delight* might indicate the opposition to war of the "con-scientious objector," took a very different stand when Nazism threatened to engulf Europe and the world. The play also marks the transition from skepticism and pessimism in regard to modern life, suggested by several of Sherwood's earlier plays, to the willingness to be engaged in political struggle and an acceptance of war, exemplified by his *Abe Lincoln in Illinois.*

Sherwood was a shrewd showman: *Idiot's Delight* gives striking evidence of this. He himself is supposed to have said, "The trouble with me is that I start off with a big message and end with nothing but good entertainment." *Idiot's Delight* was good entertainment, particularly in the acting opportunities it afforded Alfred Lunt and Lynn Fontanne, just as Leonie in *End of Summer,* in itself a charming characterization, was given special fragrance by Ina Claire's delightful talent.

John Steinbeck's *Of Mice and Men,* produced by Sam H. Harris on November 23, 1937, is a parable of American loneliness and of our hunger for "brotherhood" — two feelings the depression greatly enhanced. This play, unlike most of the others we have cited, concentrates on the unemployed of the farm lands, the itinerants and ranch workers, while it alludes to the bus and truckdrivers whose travels through the country permitted them to observe the state of the nation in its broad horizon.

The American theatre, centered in New York, is on the whole cut off from the rest of the country. The thirties was the time when the theatre, along with the other arts, rediscovered America. *Green Grow the Lilacs* (1931) is one of the several Lynn Riggs Oklahoma plays, Erskine Caldwell's *Tobacco Road* (1933), Osborn's *Morning's at Seven* (1939) — to mention only a few — are among the many which in one way or another perform a similar function. One of the reasons why Steinbeck's parable carries conviction on naturalistic grounds is that the author shares the background and the earthiness of his characters.

Steinbeck knows our longing for a home, not a mere feeding place. He has the same true sympathy for the lonesome devil whose sole companion is a mangy old dog as for the Negro cut off by his fellow workers because of his color. He suggests with something like an austere sorrow that America's "underprivileged" will never reach the home they crave till they arrive at greater consciousness.

Speaking of "austerity" I should point out that one of the ground tones of American art and theatre (particularly the latter) is sentimentality. This is also true of Steinbeck's play, though he tries to control his sentimentality. Now sentimentality is usually accounted a vice, because it bespeaks a propensity to express a greater degree of feeling than a specific situation warrants. But sentimentality need not be a vital flaw; it isn't in *Of Mice and Men.* It is often the characteristic of a young and vigorous people whose experience of life is, so to speak, still new and uncontaminated by too frequent disillusionment. In this sense our history makes us a sentimental people and it is only natural that our arts, particularly our folk arts, should reveal this quality.

William Saroyan's *The Time of Your Life* [was] presented by the Theatre Guild in association with Eddie Dowling on October 25, 1939. This sentimental comedy is by way of being a little classic. It marks the deliquescence of the aggressive mood of the thirties. For though the moralistic and critical rationale of the thirties is still present in *The Time of Your Life,* it is there in a lyrically anarchistic manner, a sort of sweet (here and there mawkish) dream.

Another way . . . of describing this play is to call it pre-beatnik! "I believe dreams more than statistics," one character says. "Everybody is behind the eight ball," says another. Money appears as the root of most evil — anyway it is the filthiest thing that goes and "there's no foundation all the way down the line," as the old man from the Orient mutters throughout the play.

In a way *The Time of Your Life* is a social fable: it turns its head away from and thumbs its nose at our monstrously efficient society which produces arrogance, cruelty, fear, headaches, constipation and the yammering of millions of humble folk, only to conclude that "all people are wonderful." Though this evinces more bewilderment than insight, it is nevertheless honestly American in its fundamental benevolence.

What saves this play, or rather what "makes" it, is its infectious humor, its anti-heroism (an oblique form of rebelliousness), its San Francisco colorfulness, its succulent dialogue, its wry hoboism and nonconformity. Though it is of another time, one still reads it with a sense of relief.

No account of the theatre of the thirties can convey any sense of its true nature and its contribution to our culture without emphasizing certain purely theatrical factors which played as decisive a role as the plays themselves.

The importance of the Group Theatre (1931–1941), whose origins may be traced back to the late twenties, can hardly be overestimated. . . . The Group Theatre was important not alone because it developed Odets from among its acting members, or even because it presented Sidney Kingsley's first play, *Men in White* (1933), Saroyan's first play, *My Heart's in the Highlands* (1939) as well as various plays by Paul Green, John Howard Lawson, Irwin Shaw and Robert Ardrey, but also because it organized its actors as a permanent company and trained them in a common craftsmanship which not only became emblematic for the era but which in many ways influenced the course of our theatre practice in the ensuing years. . . .

The Group Theatre in certain respects continued a tradition established by such pioneer organizations as the Provincetown Players, the Theatre Guild, the Neighborhood Playhouse. In another way the Group served as a model for such organizations as the Theatre Union, the Theatre Collective, the Theatre of Action, which were "workers' theatres" with a more specifically political orientation. . . . Far more important than these special organizations was the Federal Theatre Project (1935–1939) which . . . brought much excellent theatre fare to a national public at nominal prices, a public the greater part of which was barely acquainted with any form of "live" theatre. This was the first government-sponsored theatre in our history and it indicated how beneficial such an effort could be, even when circumstances were far from favorable. . . .

Looking back . . . , we may say that although admirable work still continues to be done on our constantly harassed and considerably shrunken stage, there are two virtues which may be claimed for the theatre of the thirties conspicuously lacking today. The theatre of the thirties attempted to make the stage an instrument of public enlightenment through a passionate involvement with the national scene. It made valiant and, to a remarkable degree, effective efforts to bring order and discipline into the helter-skelter of our theatre's artistic and financial organization.

An intelligent and successful Broadway producer of today recently said to me, "The theatre at present is twenty times more 'commercial' than it was in the thirties. For one thing, you could reach the hearts and souls of the actors, playwrights, designers, etc., with good sense and considerations of sound craftsmanship. Today these people, whatever their personal dispositions, appear encircled by an iron ring forged by agents who protect their clients from all thought beyond income, percentages and publicity."

The lean days and hungry nights of the thirties were a brave time. Aren't we a little torpid now?

donna gerstenberger

VERSE DRAMA IN AMERICA: 1916–1939

Verse drama has no vital tradition in the United States, for there has never been a period in the literature of this country in which verse drama has been a popular form created to express living issues. American literature had created for itself, by the end of the nineteenth century, a recognizable tradition in fiction and poetry. As the result of a number of historical factors, however, an important dramatic accomplishment came

Modern Drama, VI (December, 1963), 309–322. Reprinted by permission of the author and A. C. Edwards, editor of *Modern Drama*.

more slowly, and it was not until the period between the wars in the first half of the twentieth century that American dramatic achievement secured its place in literature. This was a period in which interest in verse drama persisted in America, and yet it was a period in which verse drama had no appreciable influence on modern American drama.

The revival of interest in a modern verse drama in England in the twenties and thirties provided an example American verse playwrights were slow to follow, perhaps because of the lack of a native tradition in the form. For the English, the sense of a major tradition of drama in verse, from Shakespeare to Milton, produced an awareness that verse for the stage could be used as a part of a vital dramatic form, even though the traditions, debased by nineteenth-century practice of blank verse, seemed something to fight free of. Interestingly enough, in its conscious attempt to free itself of the tyrannies of nineteenth-century assumptions about the romantic nature of verse drama, the English verse playwright shared the same responses that provided much of the creative energy for other contemporaneous artistic endeavors, responses which grew out of an acute awareness of having entered a new century which demanded a break with tradition and new forms of expression for new attitudes. It was more than chance, in all likelihood, that the major poets in England between the wars — Eliot, Auden, Isherwood, Spender — were also interested in the theory and practice of verse drama and that a working stage for their experiments was to be found in the Group Theatre in London.

Strangely enough, there was no comparable achievement for the verse stage in America, in spite of the influence of the general revival of interest in poetic drama as a flexible modern form. The most immediate explanation for the state of verse drama in the United States may lie in the fact that the years after the first world war saw the beginning of the first period of real influence for the drama in America, and the stage, reflecting the strongest literary influences of the post-war decades, gave itself to the service of realism. Imaginative experiments in form might be introduced, as in Elmer Rice's *The Adding Machine* or in Eugene O'Neill's *Strange Interlude,* but these experiments existed to express reality, the truth of the human situation; and prose, for the majority of American playwrights, was the adequate and appropriate vehicle for expressing reality. The reaction against Victorian or romantic attitudes included, in their minds, a reaction against verse as the language of unreality, an inherently romantic mode of expression. And the popular success of Maxwell Anderson as America's leading verse dramatist confirmed the suspicions American playwrights held about the role of verse on the stage. These feelings about verse in drama were largely justified, for, before 1935, American verse dramatists generally accepted without question the clichés of nineteenth-century verse drama.

In spite of the fact that the best energies of American playwrights were going into the realistic prose stage, there were plenty of verse dramas being written in the United States in the first third of the century. In 1916 *Poetry* magazine's contest for verse plays received some one hundred entries, with the prize going to Wallace Stevens for his *Three Travelers Watch a Sunrise,* and in January, 1918, Harriet Monroe in a *Poetry* survey of "Little Theatres and Poetic Plays" was able to report a wide interest in little theater productions of "poetic" drama, including a staging of Zoë Akins' "rather lyrical melodrama in verse," *The Magical City,* and Alfred Kreymborg's three *Plays for Poem-mimes* in St. Louis, a city which had seen a very special use of verse several years before in one of Percy MacKaye's Community Pageants, vast masque-like productions in which verse becomes a part of a general extravagance.

The most important little theatre group in America, The Provincetown Players, made room throughout the early years for an occasional verse play on their stage, although audiences on the night of November 22, 1918, must have suffered a shock when Edna St. Vincent Millay's slight one-act verse play, *The Princess Marries the Page,* was followed by Eugene G. O'Neill's *Where the Cross Is Made.* The fact that the poetess herself directed her play and performed the role of the Princess in this romantic drama (written when Millay was a Vassar undergraduate) cannot have cushioned the shock of incongruity which the second raising of the curtain must have brought.

Within the Provincetown itself, a splinter group was formed for the purpose of presenting poetic dramas, in deference to its feeling that the Provincetown was "too devoted to the kitchen sink."[1] This short-lived group, called "The Other Players," included Kreymborg and Millay, and its very existence testified to the fact that verse drama (and "poetic" theater, in general) was outside of and separate from the main efforts of the theater group which had discovered Eugene O'Neill.

Even Sidney Howard, when he tried his hand at verse drama in 1921, produced an immature, romantic costume piece, entitled *Swords* — a far cry from the theater of psychological realism he was to reach in *The Silver Cord.* The assumptions Howard made about the verse theater were those most American writers of verse plays seemed to be making, assumptions which produced into the thirties a theater not distinguishable in kind from that of the preceding century. William Vaughan Moody's drama in verse, *The Masque of Judgment,* shares the first year of the new century with the publication of Dreiser's *Sister Carrie;* but Moody's piece, typical of the standard fare of the verse theater, shares only the year with Dreiser's novel, for it looks back toward a romantic

[1] Helen Deutsch and Stella Hanau, *The Provincetown* (New York, 1931), p. 31.

tradition, while *Sister Carrie* takes its place as a part of the permanent literature of the twentieth century. There may be some excuse for the continuation of a dead tradition in Moody's verse drama in 1900, but by the middle of the thirties, with the forces active in the prose theater and in modern poetry, it is hard to explain the fact that in form, kind, attitudes, and general assumptions, American verse drama had made little progress beyond *The Masque of Judgment*.

The unquestioned assumptions generally held about drama in verse produced a theater by definition divorced from reality, a separation from reality insisted upon by the fact that the dramas inevitably took place in an historical past, peopled by costumed characters speaking a conventionalized approximation of an antique tongue; or (and there is little difference in practice) the setting is an imaginary past, the place a never-never land, with characters speaking the same conventionalized romantic language, almost always highly inflated and rhetorical, and usually in blank verse. Millay's first play, *The Princess Marries the Page* (neither the best nor the worst of the verse dramas of the period) may be illustrative, for the program for the Provincetown production carries the note: "*Time:* Some Other Time; *Place:* Somewhere Else." The action takes place in a tower and consists of a series of conversations, an unwitting courtship between a Princess and a Page who turns out, of course, to be a Prince in disguise, the heir to a neighboring kingdom, whose nasty old father conveniently dies at the end of the play.

Perhaps the most conservative of all the conventions accepted about verse drama is that which holds that the use of verse itself is a convention designed to separate the world of the stage from the world of reality; not only devoted to the unreal, the intention of verse in drama was considered to be insistently anti-realistic. As a result, the language of such plays is usually as stereotyped and unwieldy as the sweeping trains and clanking swords of the characters.

1

It may be that it was the background against which it appeared that made Wallace Stevens' verse play, the prize-winning *Three Travelers Watch a Sunrise*, seem more promising in 1916 than it does in the long view. (Stevens himself later felt that the play was "cabbage instead of the crisp lettuce intended.")[2] Like its companion play, the poetic-prose *Carlos among the Candles* (1917), *Three Travelers* is seldom, if ever, mentioned in histories of twentieth-century American drama, and it seems to have had no appreciable influence on the course of verse drama in America.

Three Travelers received little attention during its brief perform-

2 Quoted in the introduction to *Opus Posthumous* (New York, 1957), p. xxviii.

ances at the Provincetown, and the play is of interest now primarily to the students of Stevens' poetry, for it is related (like *Carlos*) to the matter of esthetics, a constant preoccupation for Stevens throughout his career. Although *Three Travelers* did not have the impact on the future of verse that the later *Sweeney Agonistes* did, Stevens at least shared with Eliot a willingness to bring to his drama the same concerns that he found worthy of serious attention in his poetry.

Stevens' play is no trifle, although it does share certain characteristics with Kreymborg's rather precious verse puppet plays; it is, at least, no variation on the theme of the Princess and the Page. In fact, *Three Travelers* exists as a serious, if often arbitrary, demonstration of an esthetic idea. As Stevens explained his intention to Harriet Monroe,

> The point of the play . . . is . . . in the last sentence of the final speech. God forbid that I should moralize. The play is simply intended to demonstrate that just as objects in nature affect us, as, for example,

> > Dead trees do not resemble
> > Beaten drums,

> so, on the other hand, we affect objects in nature, by projecting our moods, emotions, etc:

> > An old man from Pekin
> > Observes sunrise,
> > Through Pekin, reddening.[3]

Three Travelers Watch a Sunrise deserves some consideration as verse drama, for, although it did not point any new directions which could be fruitfully followed by other American verse dramatists, it did break some of the conventional rules accepted for the writing of plays in verse. But for every convention it broke, the play observed several others. One of these was its retention of the sense of remoteness, an exotic quality, not tempered by Stevens' setting of his play, which places it on an August morning, in the present time, "on a hilltop in eastern Pennsylvania." The location has no meaning for the play, and it seems as arbitrary as several other aspects of the drama, for the audience is confronted by three traveling Chinese — a pragmatist, a sage, and an esthete — all highly cultured men, who put on brightly colored robes of silk and, properly attired, await the sunrise, discoursing and singing of the prospects of wisdom and art *in vacuo* or touched by "the invasion of humanity."

The strong Symbolist influence of Stevens' early poems is evident here, and the play has about it that sense of suspended motion that one finds in Maeterlinck's plays, Mallarmé's *Herodias,* or Yeats's *The Shad-*

3 *Ibid.,* p. xxvii.

owy Waters. Humanity enters the play in the form of the two conventional Negro servants, and suffering humanity enters in the form of the dead Italian farmer and Anna, the girl before whom he has hanged himself. It is not Stevens' intention, however, that the intrusion of humanity should constitute action in the usual sense, for these two are revealed to the audience by the rising sun as a part of a tableau, as a part of the background for the real action of the play. In one sense, critics who insist that nothing happens in the play are right, although on the level of play-as-demonstration, something does, however incongruously and arbitrarily. The third Chinese, who has, throughout the discussions, insisted upon an impersonal and absolute art discovers the truth of the assertion of the second Chinese that love and wisdom come to art through its reference to the human condition:

> It is the invasion of humanity
> That counts.

Compared to the verse dramas with which it was contemporaneous, *Three Travelers* seems a guest from another world, but it is a drama destined to remain a guest on the stage, for it exists primarily as poetry rather than as drama, in spite of Stevens' assertion to Harriet Monroe that he wanted "to have the play a play and not merely a poem, if possible."[4]

2

Edna St. Vincent Millay's verse dramas found a more friendly reception on the stage than did *Three Travelers,* probably because her plays generally offered the audiences exactly what they expected of verse on the stage. For all their conventionality, several of Millay's plays do succeed in creating a conflict and engagement of human emotion (something totally lacking in Stevens' play), which, strangely enough, occurs only seldom in late nineteenth and early twentieth-century verse dramas; for, given as they are to rhetoric, such plays fail to engage, and they substitute a stereotyped and often idealized passion for human emotion. In *Aria da Capo* (1918) and *The King's Henchman* (1927), at least, Millay succeeded in creating essentially dramatic conditions, in embodying idea and emotion in action, even though the language of *The King's Henchman* never becomes anything more than a colorful adjunct to the action, reminding the audience that this is a period piece. The play was actually written, however, as an operatic libretto for Deems Taylor's music, and perhaps the only mistake was the subsequent (and highly successful) publication of *The King's Henchman* as a play in verse.

With considerable wisdom, Millay, in 1947, refused a request from

[4] *Ibid.*

her publisher to print a collection of her dramatic works. Of her seven plays, only *Aria da Capo* seemed to the author to have any enduring value — a modest judgment which most literary historians may yet feel an overestimation. *Aria da Capo* has the distinction of being one of the first (if not the first) plays in the twentieth century to use the verse stage for political comment, a use which almost wholly occupied the important writers of verse dramas in the late twenties and the thirties (cf. Auden and Isherwood, Spender, MacLeish, and Maxwell Anderson; even *Murder in the Cathedral* has its political comment to make).

In *Aria da Capo* Millay has, for the only time, sought a significant form for her drama, one which becomes a part of the total coherence of the play, and this one-act drama stands out among her other plays for this reason, although the verse is the familiar blank verse line, which serves no function except to emphasize the conventional "special" world of the verse stage. The title *Aria da Capo* — a musical term for a composition in three parts, the last being a repetition of the first — describes the form of the play, for it opens and closes with the frivolous, self-centered concerns of Pierrot and Columbine (in the ending, the cycle begins again, as in *The Bald Soprano,* with a precise repetition of the dialogue which opens the play). Between the two scenes of traditional frivolity comes the long center section, a contrast in mood and subject matter, and the insistent presence of this central material makes the mindless chatter of Pierrot and Columbine effectively inhuman (unhuman, perhaps), stressing this quality of the tradition which Millay invokes; and she succeeds for once in making the stereotype a working part of a dramatic whole. The refusal of men to leave their selfish, narrow worlds to come to terms with the threat of war and with those human characteristics which lead to war is aptly dramatized by the form of *Aria da Capo.*

The central section shows the inevitable breakdown of relations between men as the result of greed and of artificial divisions. For this section the pastoral convention is used, but beyond suggesting the allegorical intention of the play — again a convention ordinarily invoked, for distancing has an integral part in the comment the play makes — it allows the audience to see the breakdown of relationships, the operation of greed where it is least expected, where it seems least appropriate. Not even the pastoral can conceal the basic nature of man.

The two shepherds, Corydon and Thyrsis, in an enactment supervised by Cothurnus, the Masque of Tragedy, break the pastoral harmony with a seemingly-innocent division of the stage by a wall woven of colored paper ribbons. Gradually the taste of individual possession brings them to plot and accomplish each other's murder — a grim comment on the stupidity of man's greed and of his wars on others, a comment which is counterpointed by the off-stage cries of Pierrot pursuing his Pierrette.

Aria da Capo successfully breaks through the never-never land atmosphere of the majority of the verse dramas of its period by frankly accepting the stage as stage and the stereotyped characters as conventions, with the result that the form and the structure of the play, its frank theatricality, work together to make a significant comment on human experience. When Cothurnus, preempting the stage from Pierrot and Columbine, insists that the shepherds perform their parts, the objection,

> We cannot act
> A tragedy with comic properties!

and Cothurnus' answer,

> Try it and see. I think you'll find you can.
> One wall is like another.

take on a level of added significance — the tension one expects of good verse and has the right to expect of good verse drama. As Cothurnus holds the promptbook, Corydon and Thyrsis, representatives of mankind, sorrowfully admit that they are always ready to enact their murderous roles.

The accomplishment of *Aria da Capo* (concealed perhaps by its very use of the harlequinade and the pastoral) stands as an isolated incident in Millay's dramatic work, apparently suggesting no fruitful directions for her future plays. Millay's other departure from the romantic stereotype of verse drama is represented by *Conversations at Midnight* (1937), an attempt to talk over the problems and reactions of man in the modern world. But *Conversations* is a disturbing departure suggesting that at this late date the notion of verse drama as an individual and separate form with demands of its own bore no weight with Millay. One suspects that the dramatic effects of the work are best seen as being in service to what is essentially a poem (some of the speeches are sonnets, separable from the text of the work), in spite of Millay's prefatory instruction that it is best "to think of it in terms of a play" rather than as a narrative poem. The influence on *Conversations at Midnight* was apparently Robinson Jeffers' success with the narrative poem in dramatic structure in such poems as *The Tower Beyond Tragedy* and *At the Birth of an Age,* works which served Jeffers as a dramatic apprenticeship for his *Medea,* successfully staged after the conclusion of World War II.

The interest of poets in adopting dramatic structure for poems never really intended for the stage only confused the issues, but no more so than the interest of a dramatist like Maxwell Anderson in perpetuating stereotyped notions about verse on the stage. It seems a relatively simple matter now to state that neither dramatic settings for poetry nor poetic intrusions into drama create a verse drama with meaningful potential,[5] but the acceptance of this idea and the attempts to revitalize verse drama in accord with this knowledge have been both slow and painful in the twentieth century. And the example and success of Anderson has most likely hindered rather than helped such attempts in America. The most charitable and helpful conclusion may be that Anderson writes drama in which verse is used but not modern verse drama, and it is not only possible but quite logical that Denis Donoghue in his study of modern British and American verse drama, *The Third Voice* (Princeton, 1959), should effectively complete his survey without a single mention of Anderson's name. The persistence, the extensive canon in verse, and the popular reception of Anderson in the period between the wars makes Anderson a factor to be dealt with, however, even if the report, finally, is a negative one.

Anderson's theory, as well as most of his practice, quite clearly ties his verse drama to the past, for he continues unbroken the tradition which has limited the growth of verse drama in our time. Anderson's very traditional and romantic theory that "prose is the language of information and poetry the language of emotion" has led him to the use of a rhetorical verse which serves the purpose of elevation, of reminding man of his noble, if tragic, destiny. The notion that elevated expression results in elevation in the dramatic experience is in harmony with the other self-limiting conclusions that Anderson has accepted about the nature of verse drama:

> When I wrote my first play, *White Desert*, I wrote it in verse because I was weary of plays in prose that never lifted from the ground. It failed, and I did not come back to verse until I had discovered that poetic tragedy had never been successfully written about its own place and time. . . . With this admonition in mind I wrote *Elizabeth the Queen* and a succession of historical plays in verse. . . . *Winterset* is largely verse, and treats a contemporary tragic theme, which makes it more of an experiment than I could wish, for the great masters themselves never tried to make tragic poetry out of the stuff of their own times.[6]

Anderson's acceptance of the convention of the separation from reality as a principal contribution of verse in drama produced a versifying of historical events in an appropriately distanced language and verse line, in which the language, by and large, has the blurring and distancing effect of the gauze curtain AE used around the turn of the century to separate his audience from the action of his *Deirdre*. Anderson's char-

---

[5] For an example of such a statement, see my article, "Perspectives of Modern Verse Drama," *Modern Drama*, III (May, 1960), 24–29.

[6] *Off Broadway* (New York, 1947), p. 54.

acters, moving about in historic dress, speak a necessarily artificial approximation of Elizabethan blank verse, with the result that plays such as *Elizabeth the Queen, Night Over Taos, Mary of Scotland,* or *The Masque of Kings* are not distinguishable in intention and construction from the turn-of-the-century practice of verse drama. Even George Washington, in *Valley Forge,* speaks a rhetorical blank verse line which seems strangely at odds with the intention of the play to examine the evils of materialism and power politics and the temptations of dictatorship — subjects very relevant to the politically-oriented thirties but presented in an old-fashioned dress which conceals much of the immediate impact of their relevance.

Anderson's plays with contemporary settings — *Winterset, Second Overture,* and *Key Largo* (*High Tor* is costume fantasy in spite of its intruding gangsters and corrupt modern judges) — cannot be dismissed as historical dramas, and the failures of such plays to achieve a significance growing out of their use of verse suggest that Anderson's inability to create meaningful drama in verse is a basic one, not to be explained away by his preference for portraying the past on the verse stage. His failure is in the theory which leads to a preference for the past and not in the use of the historical past *per se.*

The most successful and ambitious of these contemporary plays is *Winterset,* a play of passion in which Anderson's theory of elevation calls for verse. In practice, however, the use of conventional blank verse only underlines the fact that, despite its topical subject, *Winterset* is not a modern verse drama in form or spirit.[7] Its debt to the past is summarized by Edmond M. Gagey in his *Revolution in American Drama* (New York, 1947):

> The play is less imitative of the Shakespearean form than *Elizabeth the Queen,* but . . . Anderson has absorbed much of the spirit and substance of the bard of Avon. Mio's mission of revenge for the murder of his father reminds us of *Hamlet;* Judge Guant's incoherent ravings during a thunderstorm offer a clear reminiscence of *King Lear;* Shadow, who comes back drenched and bloody from the river, is a modern counterpart of the Elizabethan ghost; the love at first sight of Mio and Mariamne [*sic.*] and their tragic situation call to mind *Romeo and Juliet.* The play has its origin, therefore, in literary tradition rather than in observation or experience, even as its dialogue is artificial and conventionalized, though it has moments of power and beauty. The catastrophe is Elizabethan in its violence but not logically convincing. (p. 84)

Although *Winterset* won the Drama Critics award for the best play of the American season, it was another play of the same year, Eliot's *Murder in the Cathedral* (presented in New York in 1936 by the Federal

---

[7] For an evaluation of the positive accomplishments of the blank verse in *Winterset,* see Joseph Wood Krutch, *American Drama Since 1918* (New York, 1957), p. 297.

Theatre), which suggested the possibility for a total coherence of verse, dramatic elements, and form, which might result in a significant verse drama. In Anderson's play the verse line is a fact of description, but it is a fact which carries little weight in the creation of a meaningful theatrical experience uniquely available in verse drama. Anderson has been called, with some justification, a prose writer who has attempted to write plays in verse[8] by Archibald MacLeish, the one American writer of verse drama in the first half century who seems to have grasped the problems involved in creating verse drama as a distinct and separate form.

If the United States has a figure in any way comparable to Eliot in concern (if not in accomplishment) for the renewal of verse drama as a modern vehicle for the stage, it has been MacLeish, a verse playwright who achieves stature in America perhaps by default. The situation might seem more promising if Eliot could be claimed for American verse drama, but this claim would clearly be the result of wishful thinking, for not only would the chronological fact of his British citizenship intervene but also the historical fact of his early association with the experimental London theater. There is no concern anywhere in his verse drama that might justify the transference of Eliot to the American score card. Such divisions between the work of English and American writers become increasingly doubtful in modern times, but in this case the distinction points up the fact that in England Eliot was working in an active community of poet-playwrights trying to create a distinctly modern verse stage, while in the United States the situation was largely stagnant, with the result that MacLeish stands pretty much alone as the only American in the period before the second world war who was willing to break verse drama away from the dominance of the past.

The period between the wars accounts, of course, only for a part of MacLeish's accomplishment, and may best, perhaps, be seen as an apprenticeship which was to lead to post-war fruition in two verse plays first produced on BBC radio — *The Trojan Horse* (1952) and *This Music Crept by Me upon the Water* (1953), the first publication of the Cambridge Poets' Theatre Series — and in the popularly-received *J.B.* (1958).

After his first and unimpressive dramatic attempt, *Nobadaddy*, MacLeish undertook the creation of topical plays in verse. The first of these was a play about the depression entitled *Panic*, which was produced by the ephemeral, experimental New York theater, The Phoenix; and *Panic* was followed by two verse plays for radio, *The Fall of the City* and *Air Raid*, both produced by the Columbia Broadcasting System with distinguished casts in 1937 and 1938 respectively. Besides writing plays in verse, MacLeish has written some valuable criticism about the prob-

[8] In *The Atlantic Monthly*, CXCV (February, 1955), 50.

lems of verse drama as a distinctive form, beginning in 1935 with his "Note on the Verse" of *Panic* and his essay, "A Stage for Poetry," an essay in which the theoretical lines are laid down for the position MacLeish expressed more fully in his 1955 essay, "The Poet as Playwright." In his early essay MacLeish establishes the terms on which verse drama must be conceived if it is to have a meaningful existence, and he explores the grounds on which he can identify Maxwell Anderson as a prose writer in verse theater in the later essay.

It is readily evident that MacLeish conceives verse drama to be a matter of special conjunction between subject, form, and language, and to this conception he adds the observation that "One certainty is that a true poetic theatre would be more realistic than the existing [prose] stage: not less." [9] This kind of serious thinking about the potentialities of verse drama reminds us of Eliot's equally serious theoretical work (although the two playwrights, in the forties, move in quite divergent directions), and MacLeish in his introductory "Note on the Verse" of *Panic* demonstrates the fact that he sees verse itself as an integral part of verse drama rather than as ornament, a pleasant adjunct – a concept which makes the "Note on the Verse" more important in some ways than the play itself, for the play is relatively unsuccessful in its attempt to define and dramatize an attitude toward the American depression. In his note, MacLeish begins by rejecting blank verse as inappropriate to the speech of Americans in the twentieth century: "as a vehicle for contemporary expression it is pure anachronism," because "the rhythm of blank verse and the rhythms of the spoken language of our country are precisely opposed." For our purposes, the fact that MacLeish should question the traditional line is more important than the accuracy of his conclusions, although his ideas about American speech are interesting in themselves, and they provide the rationale on which the verse of *Panic* is built, a line of five accents but unlimited syllables, with a descending rhythm opposed to the pattern of blank verse.

The other experiment which MacLeish makes is the attempt to use the broken comments of the crowd in the street in place of a chorus – a practice also present in a lesser degree in the two radio plays he wrote in the thirties. It is tempting to deal with these plays for radio in some detail, particularly since they have received actual stage performance also, but perhaps the most important thing about the plays is the impulse which turned MacLeish toward the concept of the verse play for radio. Most important to MacLeish was the elimination of such matters as setting and visible actors in favor of "the word-excited imagination."

---

[9] "A Stage for Poetry," *A Time to Speak* (Boston, 1941), p. 80.

On the stage, verse is often an obstacle because the artifice of the verse and the physical reality of the scene do not harmonize: it is for this reason that verse is easily accepted on the stage only where the scene is made remote in time and therefore artificial to begin with, or where the verse is blurred out and made to sound as much as possible like prose.[10]

MacLeish's solution was only a partial one, but his desire to restore the impact of word and rhythm to verse drama is comparable to the motivation which sent Yeats to the aristocratic Noh theater, where all is simple ritual and where it is "the word-excited imagination" which creates.

MacLeish also saw radio as an answer to the absence of any commercial theater in the United States in the late thirties where the verse play might find a stage, and radio it seemed, was a way of finding and building in America a relatively large audience for verse plays. (It is interesting, in this context, to find MacLeish admitting in 1953 that commercial radio and its promise of audiences for verse drama had been an insubstantial hope, a failure which turned MacLeish, temporarily it would seem, toward the kind of special audience provided by The Poets' Theatre — a direction which MacLeish, turning away from the promise of a popular hearing for verse theater, identifies with that which Yeats took late in his life as the result of a similar reaction and parallel failure to create the kind of theater he wanted among the people.)[11]

The Fall of the City is easily the best of MacLeish's plays of the thirties, a play in which his attempt to use a special resource of radio, the announcer, provides a natural commentator who can fulfill and expand the function of the chorus. *The Fall of the City* lends itself nicely to the impersonal, semi-documentary technique of the reporter, for it dramatizes a political theme, the fall of a people to a conqueror they have created out of their own nameless dread and their desire to be mastered. The verse of this play is extremely flexible and functional, often using short, nervous lines to express the *angst* of the modern world that recall Auden's verse for similar themes.

MacLeish's radio plays offer no permanent solution to the problems of creating a modern verse drama, but they do explore some possible directions for American verse playwrights. The fact that radio performance was no guarantee of successful verse drama is demonstrated by Kreymborg's 1938 play, *The Planets,* which, despite its dedication to peace, is a fantasy made up of masque-like elements, set into motion by an astrologer, who, after surveying the sad state of earth, is miraculously transported to outer space, where he converses with various heavenly bodies. The verse is more integral and operative than that in Kreymborg's earlier poem-mimes, but there is nothing in *The Planets* to add

---

10 *The Fall of the City* (New York, 1937), p. x.
11 Foreword, *This Music Crept by Me upon the Waters* (Cambridge, Mass., 1953).

to an estimate of the possibilities for a viable verse drama in the United States.

That possibilities for the creation of verse drama exist has been amply demonstrated in the period following the second world war, a twenty-year period which saw a growth of significant activity, primarily among poets like Cummings, MacLeish, Frost, and Eberhardt, to name a few. For some, the earlier period between the wars provided apprentice years, and perhaps it is a period which receives justice only if considered as an exploratory period, a period reluctant to move verse drama forward, out of a dead tradition, until the traditional had been sufficiently explored by American playwrights. Whatever the explanation, the period between the wars was far from being a golden age for verse drama in America, but it may yet be seen as a period in which the refining fires were at work, burning away a great deal of dross.

edith j. r. isaacs

LILLIAN HELLMAN: A PLAYWRIGHT ON THE MARCH

The ranks of America's practising playwrights have thinned out even more than might have been expected since the war began. Among those who are left only two can be said to have grown notably in stature, Moss Hart and Lillian Hellman. *Winged Victory* will speak proudly for Moss Hart. . . . The success of *Watch on the Rhine* is recent enough to serve as witness to Lillian Hellman's progress, and the story can still be found, with equal dramatic effect, in the movies, running almost alongside this author's newest film, *The North Star*.

It is just nine years since Lillian Hellman burst into attention with *The Children's Hour*, a bitter play about two young women whose lives were wrecked by a sadistic child and a careless old woman. The author was more fortunate than most playwrights in having a wise director, Herman Shumlin, and a fine cast for her first play. Most of the players

Theatre Arts, XXVIII (January, 1944), 19–24. Copyright 1944 by Theatre Arts, Inc. Reprinted by permission of Hermine I. Popper.

were women — the only man's role of any importance was Dr. Cardin, played by Robert Keith. The leading parts — the head of a girls' school and her associate — were excellently portrayed by Katherine Emery and Anne Revere. But there was another character that shared the spotlight with them and that seemed at certain points to blot out everything except the blackness of her particular little evil soul or what passed for her soul. Remembering the play, it is hard to say whether it was Lillian Hellman's creation of this character, or Florence McGee's acting, or the summation of falsity, depravity and cruelty represented by this child — the source of all disaster — that focussed the thoughful, but not entirely friendly, notice of critics and public alike upon the unusual, skilful, extravagantly unpleasant work before them. The play left no doubt of the talent that lay behind it. It had the essential elements of good drama — plot, character, conflict, movement, and words that were vibrant and active, good theatre words. But in some not quite explicable way the writing lacked artistic discipline. In spite of the author's clear gifts of invention it was obvious that the playwright had a stubborn mind and a determination to go her own way, and to go it alone if necessary, whatever obstacles man and art might put in her path. And that is a bad fault in a dramatist whose works can come to life on a stage only through the understanding and sympathetic cooperation of actors and directors. Almost invariably it makes a writer work too hard to secure his effects, and paradoxically it often belittles the effects.

Today Lillian Hellman has to her credit plays as good as *The Little Foxes* and *Watch on the Rhine*, works of her own and others translated into films with outstanding success, and now another film, *The North Star*, opening to drumbeats and hosannas. Nine years have given her a record of mastery over difficult situations and unfamiliar stage characters only once interrupted by the failure of *Days to Come*. Yet all this success has not cured her of her major limitation. She still works too hard. She gives generous praise to the friends who have helped her, but the one thing these friends seem not to have told her or not to have told her effectively is to relax, to trust herself and her fellow-workers more.

The reason Lillian Hellman overworks is clear. She lacks faith in the theatre as a medium and especially in her audience. And it may well be that only the movies — the grave of much playwriting talent — will finally remedy that fault. For a playwright who tries to do the work of his actors and the thinking of his audience may sometimes get away with it if enough other elements combine in his favor. But the scriptwriter who does not trust the camera to do half the job is beaten before he begins. Working with the films may be the secret influence that made *The Little Foxes* and *Watch on the Rhine* so much better than *The Children's Hour,* so infinitely better than *Days to Come.*

In the introduction to her *Four Plays,* Miss Hellman tells of reading the proofs of these plays and of finding many things wrong. She is more modestly critical of her accomplishment than most writers would be and yet she does not always seem to know what the "real wrong th'ng" is. She says, for example, "The theatre has limitations: it is a tight, unbending, unfluid, meagre form in which to write. And for these reasons, compared to the novel, it is a second-rate form. Let us admit that. Having admitted it . . . we can stop the pretentious lie that the stage is unhampered." But who is going to admit that? Every part is limited by its form and range, painting by flat canvas, sculpture by the density and grain of the stuff with which it works. All art is discipline. It must make its own adjustment between creative imagination on the one side and reality on the other. The fact that the theatre is not unhampered does not make it a second-class medium, but only an art that requires great care in the selection and arrangement of its materials.

Again Miss Hellman complains, not unjustifiably, that too many critics have objected to her plays as melodramatic because they are violent (there is at least one violent death in every play) and says that we have lost much of the value of the word "melodrama" by applying it to plays that "use its violence for no purpose, to point no moral. . . . When violence is actually the needed stuff of the work and comes toward a large enough end, it has been and always will be in the good writer's field." She is right there, only — until *Watch on the Rhine* — she seemed to miss the point that while the violence of a playwright's action may be suited to his own desire and his own needs, yet if he makes an actor say something violently which might be said more effectively if said more simply, he weakens his speech, and if he heightens a character beyond the point at which a good actor can present a living portrait, he undoes his own handiwork. More faith in her actors would not interfere with the violence of Miss Hellman's action, which so far is a central facet of her technique, but would prevent her heightening her characters, apparently in the mistaken hope that if the actor did not do his whole job the author's intention would still be clear.

So far as the audience is concerned, no playwright ever focussed them into action by turning stump speaker. "I am a moral writer," Miss Hellman says, "often too moral a writer, and I cannot avoid, it seems, that last summing-up. I think that is only a mistake when it fails to achieve its purpose, and I would rather make the attempt, and fail, than fail to make the attempt." That is honest indeed but it is not wise. As a belligerent moralist, what Miss Hellman most wants of her audience is undoubtedly that they should go out and act more generously, more socially, more nobly because of what her play sets forth. But with her experience she should know that you cannot drive a theatre audience to shoulder a gun for a cause or even to sign on the dotted line as they leave the house just because you have dinned your moral into their ears. They are far more apt to be moved to action the next day or the next week if, remembering the play in tranquillity, they think up the moral afresh and imagine themselves to be acting on their own impulse.

In Giraudoux's *Impromptu de Paris,* which he wrote for Jouvet's company some years ago, he lets Jouvet say:

> When I see a member of the audience sitting on the edge of his seat, straining to understand what the author means, trying to make sense out of every one of our words, gestures, intonations, I feel like going to the footlights and saying: "Don't take it so hard, my dear fellow. Relax. You'll understand everything tomorrow. . . . Get a good sleep and in the morning you'll know. If you wake up feeling heavy, dull, disgusted with your job — the play is bad. But if you feel buoyant, happy, filled with ardor, with noble indignation, with tenderness — the play is good."

The theatre is not arithmetic but magic. That is the essence of sound theatre philosophy.

Lillian Hellman's plays are about different people in quite different situations. *Days to Come* is about a strike in a "model" town. Its characters are a confused array of workers, employers, strike leaders, strike breakers and idle, neurotic women. In *The Little Foxes* a scheming, greedy, ruthless, newly-rich family in a lazy, Southern neighborhood occupies centre-stage, with an ineffectual Southern gentlewoman, an unhappy child and a kindly old Negro servant acting as contrast. *Watch on the Rhine* is of this war, with a fashionable suburb of Washington as its arena. Its characters are less like symbols and more like people than the men and women of the earlier plays. A German scientist (a fighter in the underground army and Lillian Hellman's most heroic portrait) is the central figure and around him are grouped his family, his wife's family — their hosts — and a Rumanian spy.

But however different the story, the place and the people, the theme of Miss Hellman's play is always the same, the struggle between good and active evil, between evil and good that are sometimes ignorant of themselves, sometimes in full knowledge of what they are. It takes creative skill and technical equipment to approach a single goal from many angles and still to keep each separate line of approach clear, each story vivid. The single-minded devotion to her own idea of what is important today and her ability to translate the idea into play form over and over again with an increasing power and persuasion are Lillian Hellman's distinctive achievement.

Exactly what this idea is she says in two closely related speeches. The first is from *The Little Foxes* where old Addie, "a tall, nice-looking Negro woman, about fifty-five", a family retainer, says:

> There are people who eat the earth and eat all the people on it like in the Bible with the locusts. Then there are people who stand around and watch them eat it. Sometimes I think it ain't right to stand and watch them do it.

The second is from *The North Star*. Old Dr. Kurin, the devoted scientist and physician who has served the little Russian village which is the protagonist of the film, finds a famous German surgeon, whom he knew as a student, taking children's blood (so much that they die from it) for transfusion to wounded Germans. Kurin goes into the room where Dr. Von Harden and his assistant, Richter, a typical Nazi, are operating. He says to Von Harden:

> I have heard about men like you. The civilized men who are sorry. That (*points to Richter*), that kind is nothing. They will go when their bosses go. But men like you who have contempt for men like him, to me *you* are the real filth. Men who do the work of Fascists and pretend to themselves they are better than those for whom they work. Men who do murder while they laugh at those who order them to do it. (*With great anger*) It is men like you who sold your people to men like him.

The core of all the social anger which is the driving force in Miss Hellman's dramas is contained in those two speeches: "Sometimes I think it ain't right to stand around and watch them do it." — "Civilized men who are sorry. . . . Men who do murder while they laugh at those who order them to do it." It is the plea for an active, fighting, total goodness (toward which words and ideas count little and only brave deeds make a real contribution). It is not only the foundation but almost the entire structure of *The North Star*, with its idyllic setting of the Russian village which opens the film against the holocaust which ends it.

But again *Watch on the Rhine* stands out as the work in which the means and the end are most thoroughly blended. The Fascist evil is set against the glowing bravery of the underground, personified not only in Kurt Müller but in his family. And here the author's theme is stated again, simply and directly:

> KURT. I have no wish to make a mystery of what I have been doing; it is only that it is awkward to place neatly. It sounds so big; it is so small. I am an Anti-Fascist. And that does not pay well. . . .
> FANNY. Are you a radical?
> KURT. You would have to tell me what that word means to you, Madame.
> FANNY (*after a slight pause*). That is just. Perhaps we all have private definitions. We all are Anti-Fascists, for example —

SARA. Yes. But Kurt works at it.
FANNY. What kind of work?
KURT. Any kind. Anywhere.

Moreover, the whole action of *Watch on the Rhine* stems from the characters themselves and their relations to the world around them. The distance Miss Hellman has travelled since *The Children's Hour* is marked by the fact that in *Watch on the Rhine* she has not only a theme and a story arranged to suit her moral purpose but leading characters who have learned to speak for themselves.

Almost every creative novelist and playwright has had the experience of having certain of his characters suddenly do and say things beyond his conscious intentions for them. They take on a life of their own and at times their speeches seem to come only through the author's fingertips. That happens only when the characters are alive and integrated in the author's mind, not when they are his puppets. Kurt Müller speaks for himself and so does his wife Sara. Yet there is no doubt, knowing Miss Hellman and her philosophy, that she likes what they say, that it is exactly what she would have them say. In fact, there is no proof that she did not hammer out each sentence they speak as painstakingly as she did the speeches in her early plays or that she did not know exactly what she was writing at each stroke. No proof except the fact that these people are alive and that they set us aquiver with their actions and their emotions, as characters do who have their own life.

Miss Hellman is beginning to relax. We wait with eager attention for her next play.

travis bogard

THE COMEDY OF THORNTON WILDER

The theater is the natural home of the cliché. Stereotypes of character, situation, and belief which a novelist would be embarrassed to conceive, much less develop, come to their particular fulfillment in the

From *Three Plays by Thornton Wilder*, Harper and Row, New York, 1962. Copyright © 1962 by Travis Bogard. Reprinted by permission of the publisher.

theater. Only at the theater is one treated so frequently to innocent adulteries, and guilt-ridden matrimonial triangles, to psychopathic villains terrorizing the incipiently courageous, to drifters questing for mothers who have betrayed them, to homespun philosophers crackling with rural wisdom, to melodramatized conflicts between dark and light, right and left, vice and virtue. Only at the theater is experience formulated in terms of repetitive stylizations of human behavior and accepted with so little effective question.

At its worst, the theatrical cliché beggars insight, heating the theater with false passion, with concepts empty of thought, and with attitudes that have been assumed for the occasion without reference to morality or to psychology. The bulk of drama, prefabricated from this rotten timber, crumbles, and what survives is so jerry-built, so patched and misshapen that it can command no real respect from those to whom art is more than a plaything. The phenomenon of antidrama, Ionesco's *The Bald Soprano,* for instance, indicates the degree of revulsion and contempt which even dramatists themselves feel for a genre which, in large part, is so essentially mindless.

The drama may indeed be dismissed as the subliterary toy of the director and actor who have power to divert audiences in spite of the cliché-ridden script. Yet even the greatest drama is not proof against the cliché. In many instances, major playwrights appear to find solid timber in the rubble of stereotypical theatrical patterns. The tedious, routine story of the revenger told repeatedly in the late Elizabethan theater peaked in Shakespeare's treatment to *Hamlet;* the sophisticated and cynical man-of-the-world who unexpectedly falls in love — such staple fare of the comedy of the Restoration — becomes Congreve's Mirabel; the wife's choice of a lover or husband — the dusty furniture of so many plays by Arthur Wing Pinero and Henry Arthur Jones — becomes, when Shaw develops it, *Candida;* and the mother-questing hero — that common coin of the American dramatist — becomes in O'Neill's work Eben Cabot and Edmund Tyrone.

The great dramatist uses, rather than avoids, the cliché, turning it into a source of strength for his purposes. He is not dominantly an innovator in his themes or his methods. His novelties are in his attitudes, as with Shaw, his finesse, as with Congreve, his intensity, as with Shakespeare and O'Neill. In an art form partaking of ritual and ceremony, the chief strength lies not in novelty, but in the symbolic patterns which involve playwright, performers and audience in a kind of communion. Cliché, carefully developed, can serve as myth serves, to establish a basis of belief.

A dramatist must do more than give new names to old situations. He must not merely accept them, but must search them for their human roots. He must fit them into a larger concept of his action so that they do more than thrill cheaply the emotions of the spectator. The best balance sets character as both individual and symbol, exploring in a given situation the dilemmas of the individual man and the meaning he has in a larger scheme of implication. In establishing both the immediate and the general, the cliché character and situation are often serviceable as connecting points, for they base themselves on possible human actions; at the same time, because they have been used in so many dramas, they suggest an archetypical possibility through which the largest significance of the action may be developed.

Thornton Wilder has been highly praised as an innovator, a man who, along with O'Neill, freed the American theater from its traditional forms through his experiments in *Our Town* and *The Skin of Our Teeth*. Quite properly, he may be placed in parallel with Bertolt Brecht as a dramatist who uses the technique of alienation to develop an anti-illusory, openly theatrical theater. In *The Skin of Our Teeth* and many of the short plays which preceded it, there are anticipations of such a seemingly new theatrical style as that developed by Tennessee Williams in *Camino Real*. At some moments, he seems to be writing anti-drama in a manner anticipatory of Ionesco. Yet, at the center of all his dramatic work — indeed almost as its major structural element — lies the cliché.

Compared with his drama, Wilder's novels seem fresh-minted, new conceptions whose effects are not repeated. In his novel *The Woman of Andros* (1930), he describes the return of a dead hero from the underworld to relive an ordinary day in his fifteenth year. "Suddenly, the hero saw that the living too are dead and that we can only be said to be alive in those moments when our hearts are conscious of our treasures; for our hearts are not strong enough to love every moment. And not an hour had gone by before the hero who was both watching life and living it called on Zeus to release him from so terrible a dream. The gods heard him, but before he left he fell upon the ground and kissed the soil of the world that is too dear to be realized."

Wilder developed the same suggestion for the climactic moment of *Our Town,* but in the play when Emily returns from the dead to relive a day when she was totally happy, there is instantly summoned to mind dozens of sentimental dramatic romances such as *The Return of Peter Grimm, Smiling Through,* and J. M. Barrie's *Mary Rose.* In the drama the quality of the novel's situation is altered. What was new becomes stereotyped; and yet, with a paradox that can only be resolved by a consideration of the difference between novel and drama, it is Emily who is remembered, just as it is through his dramas, rather than his novels, that Wilder's reputation has become international.

Wilder's earliest dramatic work was published in 1928, following the success of his novel, *The Bridge of San Luis Rey*. In a volume entitled *The Angel that Troubled the Waters*, he collected sixteen one-act plays, some so brief as to be scarcely visible. Many are less than scenes of five minutes' duration. Were it not that each centers firmly on a moral conflict, the plays would more properly be called "Imaginary Conversations" than drama. Yet, although brief and experimental, they are not trivial.

The scope of their conception is astonishing. The *dramatis personae* of the volume include Christ, Satan, Judas and Gabriel; a French dancer and her tubercular husband; Mary, Joseph and Hepzibah, the talkative donkey bearing the Holy Family into Egypt; St. Francis; a great actress and her lover; a mermaid; Ibsen, Shelley, Mozart and Childe Roland. Scenically, were a designer to take Wilder's stage directions literally, each play would require a setting of staggering expense: heaven, hell, the bottom of the sea, a pool in an oriental mosque. A five-page play called *And the Sea Shall Give Up Its Dead* opens with this stage direction:

> The clangor of Judgment Day's last trumpet dies away in the remotest pocket of space, and time comes to an end like a frayed ribbon. In the nave of creation the diaphanous amphitheater is already building for the trial of all flesh. Several miles below the surface of the North Atlantic, the spirits of the drowned rise through the water like bubbles in a neglected wine glass.

In no way, except in their essential conflict, are the majority of these plays fit for, or intended for, the theater. They are exercises of unusual kinds, which Wilder, as he makes clear in his preface, constructed for his amusement to satisfy his curiosity in matters of literature and humanity. Yet they are the beginning, and their quality should be marked.

Their elaborate production schemes, so disproportionate to their length, reflect an unconcern for the routine practices and limitations of the realistic theater. Stripped of embellishments they reduce to very simple elements: to the "three boards and a passion" called for as a prime dramatic essential by older dramatists. In essence they are most like the dramas of the cyclical medieval religious dramas, uncomplicated in their psychology, deceptively naive, and permitting, though not requiring, elaborate production schemes.

They are not especially concerned with characterization as that term, post-Freud, has called for intricate exploration of psychological motivation. They center, instead, on situation and the emotion emerging from the conflict it engenders. The externals of character are sufficiently revealed to provide human habitation for emotion and no more. Man is viewed at a distance, *sub species aeternitatis*, and in this long view much particularizing detail drops from him.

None of these short works is cheap or sentimental. A conversation between Mary, Joseph and their garrulous, spinsterish donkey is saved from frightful excesses of cuteness and sentimentality by its brevity, by its native wit, and by Wilder's refusal to permit his actors to provide the characters with more reality of emotion than his design calls for.

This play, *The Flight into Egypt,* can be taken as typical of Wilder's work, and as anticipatory of his later, more mature dramaturgy. Mary, riding on the donkey Hepzibah with Joseph at her side, carries the Christ child toward Egypt. The donkey, refusing to hurry even when the clashing armor of Herod's pursuing soldiers sounds from the wings, talks incessantly, of her legs and theology and points of interest on the route. Behind her, the scenery unrolls on a revolving cyclorama, like the vistas in the mechanical wonders of a Dime Museum. The Tigris and Euphrates pass by; then the pyramid and the Sphinx; and it is only when the Donkey realizes that Mary carries the child who was born in the stable where she was formerly tethered that she hurries and completes the journey successfully.

Clearly this is dangerous ground for a dramatist. It is a combination of cliché concepts assembled in a way that to audiences trained in realistic theater might seem novel. Yet the treadmill on which Hepzibah walks and the unrolling scenery were staple commodities of the nineteenth century spectacles, such as *Ben Hur;* the balky donkey is comic strip material even today, and the talkative spinster who becomes capable in a crisis is routine theatrical fare. The application of these elements to Christian story is the only novelty, and this, in view of the play's evidently traditional moral, is unimportant.

The effect of the whole when it is produced is exactly as Wilder's scenic description suggested it should be: a charming mechanical toy, which when wound tightly and the proper springs pressed, endlessly reiterates its story. Character does not obtrude on the sense of the remote and the miniature. The machinery of the setting and the cliché characterizations prohibit any particularization. The Holy Family is separated artfully from reality, held at a distance, turned by Wilder's control of the cliché into myth. Compared with the tedious amateurism of many of the experimental one-act plays of the early twentieth century American theater, *Flight into Egypt,* like its companion plays, reveals a young dramatist with an instinctive mastery of theatrical essentials.

In 1931, six more ambitious one act plays appeared in the volume *The Long Christmas Dinner.* It is an uneven volume. Three of the plays, *Queens of France, Love, and How to Cure It,* and *Such Things Only Happen in Books* suggest that Wilder made some effort to come to terms with the theater as he found it and to work with relatively realistic techniques. The results are charming in certain romantic details and amusing in their tricks of plots, but the plays seem slight beside such shorter works as *The Flight into Egypt.*

The remaining half of the volume is of a different order. Taking his direction from the first little plays, Wilder affirmed what was to become his characteristic dramatic manner and found ways to increase the emotional and thematic substance without losing scope or imaginative freedom. The plays in question are the title play, *The Happy Journey to Trenton and Camden,* and *Pullman Car Hiawatha.*

Like *Flight into Egypt,* each of these longer plays is a journey play. *The Long Christmas Dinner* does not move in space, but involves a progress through time, as a family's several generations act their typical stories around a Christmas-dinner table — being born, maturing, and dying at a ninety year long ceremonial feast. *The Happy Journey* describes a motor trip from Newark to Camden, New Jersey, and *Pullman Car Hiawatha* encompasses a night's train trip from New York to Chicago.

Flight into Egypt, like its companion plays, required an elaborate production scheme to achieve the distance and the freedom in space and time. For these later plays the requirement remains, but the theatrical means are refined and simplified. The primary restriction on space, time, and distance in drama is setting. If there is furniture, it must be used; if people live in houses, they must relate to its windows and doors; if visual reality is desired in a production, then the characters must also seem real and work as real people do, within the bounds of seemingly real time and place. But if this is not the end, then setting and furniture can be dispensed with, and, with a stroke, the problem is solved.

The Long Christmas Dinner has a purely functional setting: the table and chairs of the dinner itself and two portals, one through which characters enter as they are born, the other the portal to death. Setting is here reduced and turned to symbol with a simple theatrical directness reminiscent of the door to the grave in the medieval morality play, *Everyman.* Undetailed and stark, the setting establishes no limit to the play's sense of the passing of years, and it requires no more than token use by the actors whose common mortality is more vital than their traits of character as individuals.

The settings of *Pullman Car Hiawatha* and *The Happy Journey* are more openly theatrical, less symbolic. In these, the stage is stripped. A platform with lights and chairs, plus a few flats to insist visually that the stage *is* a stage replace the trappings of ordinary theatrical illusions. Here, for the first time in Wilder's work, the Stage Manager is brought before the audience to arrange the furnishings, to describe the effect the setting is supposed to have, and to sustain in his own person the concept of non-illusory drama, which permits the plays to describe their journeys.

What led Wilder to develop these devices is less to the purpose than the consequences of such innovations. A boyhood in the Orient had undoubtedly taught him something of the freedom and scope of the oriental drama, and had perhaps conditioned him to the charming utilitarian values of the formalized acting styles and the ubiquitous, visible-invisible functionaries allied to his Stage Manager. Similarly, his interest in theater would have led him to consider the value of the expressionist experiments of the followers of Strindberg. In the same years as he wrote, the theatrical waters were stirred with experiments similar to his. In Germany, Bertolt Brecht was becoming acquainted with Oriental theater and adapting its methods to his style of Epic Theater. In America, the experiments of O'Neill, John Howard Lawson, and many others had suggested the possibility and the desirability of a break from the realistic unities of Ibsen.

Yet, as his first collection suggested, if Wilder were to write drama at all he would have to move toward a nonrealistic dramatic manner. The development of such enabling techniques was essential so long as he held to his attempt to depict the individual in terms that would call to mind the ultimate destiny of all mankind. And this was his theme. In a sense, perhaps, all of Wilder's plays are about the Day of Judgment, imaging human character as a bubble rising to burst on the surface of eternity. There undoubtedly were influences on his experimental style, but, in the last analysis, Wilder's innovations are important consequences of his point of view and of his way of commenting on experience.

The results of the stylistic developments are important. To take *Pullman Car Hiawatha* as a single example: As the train runs westward through the night, like the mechanical Tigris and Euphrates in *The Flight into Egypt,* fields and towns (including Grover's Corners, Ohio) appear and state their relation to it; trackworkers and others concerned with the train's operation step forward to speak their pieces, like graduates of a School of Elocution, awkwardly stilted in speech, paralyzed with stage-fright; and ultimately, guided by the Stage Manager, the hours of the night and the planets pronounce, through wise saws of the ages, a kind of benediction on the train and its passengers, who restlessly mutter their night thoughts. The sense is of many voices, half heard at a distance, joining in a chorus somehow relevant to man's destiny, somehow in harmony with the singing planets and with a vast but living immensity. In the end, the train does not click along tracks to a purely local destination. It becomes part of the entire westering turn of the earth, part of the movement of life in space.

The production scheme permits Wilder to hold a view of man that takes into account individual differences, but in the end reduces them in size. Characters are sufficiently drawn to reveal particular human dilemmas, yet nothing that anyone does is important in its own right. Again, the human characters are cliché figures, but as their individual characteristics slip from them, as their passions are shown to be symptomatic of the kinds of emotions each of these kinds of people would feel, and as individual will remains powerless before final destiny, the cliché figures form into a pattern whose sense is of a typical assortment of men and women, no one worthier of attention than any other. Because they are cliché images of men, they hold an anonymity entirely suitable to Wilder's larger design.

This is not to say that man is unimportant in the total design. If anything, his importance is increased in relation to the wide scheme against which he is projected. Man's will, passion, and suffering, however, are not his most important characteristics. Rather, his importance emerges through his relationship with nature's cyclic movement. He is measured by what he touches, rather than by what he does, and these points of wide-ranging contact are only revealed by maintaining the broadest perspective on his action. Through this perspective, the dramatist found his most characteristic means of expressing his sense of life, and it may have been these means, the theatrical cliché combined with a startlingly simplified stagecraft, that permitted him to become — in his full-length plays — the only important American writer of comedy.

In comedy, when it has not been scraped and sharpened by an informing satiric intelligence, man is shown as the inhabitant of a basically benevolent world. The sense is that he lives within a charmed circle where nothing ultimately painful or evil can happen. The man who slips on the banana peel does not damage his sacroiliac, lovers forced to spend a damp and foggy night on the ground in a wood near Athens do not suffer from over-exposure, heartbreak returns to laughter, and *hubris* leads only to a reasonable acceptance of society's norms. The benevolent limits on action and its consequences affect character, as well. The range of emotion in comedy tends to be smaller. Passionate outbursts with far-reaching consequences, pain, even violent excesses of love are gentled, narrowed, reduced in size and kind and rendered more artificial than real.

In Wilder's first full-length play, *Our Town* (1938) the techniques of the comic artist emerge clearly. The characters are limited, held within the benevolent social framework of a turn-of-the-century small town. Their ambitions are unimportant, their suffering is never great and its consequences are muted. They do not quarrel nor lust. They have no thought for their past or their future. They are bounded by reassuring statistical summaries, by familiar occurrences — the night train, the round of the milkman and the paperboy, the homeward stumbling of the drunken organist — and by familiar places — the kitchen, the soda fountain, the graveyard on the hill.

Significantly, they do not look beyond this bounded township at the nation, the world-at-large, nor at the universal scheme in which they figure. They are not inquirers into destiny, and it is clear that nothing they say or do will ever attempt to alter the nature of things. Instead, they maintain the daily, pious rounds of activity, keeping place within set limits. The result is that they are not called upon to express passion of any violent kind, nor are they permitted to cry out in pain. Wilder removes from his stage even scenes of sickness, although instances are reported in passing. Thus, without important action of will, curiosity or awareness, Wilder's characters are brought to a condition of emotional gentleness. At its farthest range, their wonder achieves only a childlike awe at the concept expressed in an envelope's address:

> Jane Crofut
> The Crofut Farm
> Grover's Corners
> Sutton County
> New Hampshire
> The United States of America
> Continent of North America
> Western Hemisphere
> The Earth
> The Solar System
> The Mind of God

To Rebecca Gibbs, who tells of the letter, what is most remarkable is that "the postman brought it just the same."

It is odd, perhaps, that these inherently docile creatures, incapable of heroism or villainy, are not to be blamed for refusing to attempt to shape their destinies, but Wilder protected his villagers from a charge of spinelessness partly by admitting no occasion to test them. Later, in *The Skin of Our Teeth*, where every moment is a crisis of huge dimension, Wilder buries the individual response in farcical vaudeville, again relieving the characters from becoming involved as individuals in any moral or spiritual dilemmas. What is left in *Our Town* moves perilously close to the sentimental, and would perhaps commit itself irrevocably to saccharine patriotic images were it not that Wilder measures humanity from a distance.

The essential difference between *Our Town* and the bulk of American folk drama is that Wilder attempts to convince no one of his truth by insisting that what he presents is the reality itself. If his story had been developed realistically, carefully plotted, decorated so as to attempt to convince the audience that it was seeing living human beings, much of its truth would have drained from the play, and all of it would have seemed sentimental and unconvincing. But Wilder, as his earlier plays suggested he might, avoids this and with it much of the fraudulence of American folk drama. He insists that the actors are only pretending to be characters. They are stage-managed; they are in rehearsal, so to speak. Above

all, they are not attempting to convince anyone of the reality of their illu-
sionary comings and goings. They are deliberately depicted as theatrical
stereotypes.

The result is that Wilder's characters become emblems of reality, not
reality itself. They are there to remind audiences of familiar things in
whose recognition there is pleasure and security. Like the statistics
quoted in the opening sequences of the play, the things the characters do
are ways of naming blessings.[1] The characters seem a little like priests,
the guardians of a shrine whose rituals they only dimly comprehend. In
their appointed rounds, they touch familiar things and receive a kind of
blessing from the act. They are secure in eternity, and what they do is a
ritual enactment of realities which do not need analysis. And because
they are deliberate artifices, they escape the merely sentimental. What
they touch has the power of a propitiatory charm, a tribal totem, warding
off any invasion of evil or doubt.

The distance provided by the artifice permits the drama to move
through broken scenes, fragmentarily tracing the lives of George and
Emily and their families and their neighbors. Its primary emotion is the
joy of discovery and remembering the discovery of the limited world.
Moving backward and forward in time and place, the scenes form, in the
end, a whole and describe man's course in the timeless cycle of eternity.
Even the moment of greatest agony, when Emily returns to earth and
cries out that man is unaware of joy as it passes, diminishes in the free
slip of time. Tears drain into the earth and memory lies light as the flesh
disappears and as thought releases its hold on dead limbs.

For an audience, this is the value of the play: that it reminds men
of the good underlying their hesitation, doubts and agony. It promises
no salvation, but, equally, in *Our Town* no one is damned. Wilder does
not deny the reality of suffering, the necessity of questing and inquiry,
but he sees that all such passion and acts of will shall pass away in the
surcease of eternity.

In *Our Town*, the open theatricalism acts to diminish the sentimental cliché latent in the subject matter in much the same way that the
convention of the boy actress permitted the artificial and improbable
plotting of *As You Like It* to become effective. Character is kept at a
distance by the stress on the theatrical means. In *Our Town*, the device
obviates the necessity for sustained narrative and, while still permitting
character to move and to hold an audience's interest, reduces it to some-

---

[1] Detailed biographical evidence is lacking in substantiation, but his plays suggest that
Wilder himself touched reality as firmly and as often as he could. For instance, in *The Happy
Journey to Trenton and Camden* he names a high school principal, Mr. Biedenbach, who was
in fact the principal of the Berkeley (California) High School which Wilder attended. In
the same play, the characters pass and comment on the Lawrenceville Academy where Wilder
was teaching as he wrote the play. A sudden blurring of artifice and reality occur, as if the
characters were watching Wilder watching them.

thing like norms of the experience Wilder is presenting.

In *The Merchant of Yonkers* (1938), Wilder experimented with another device for attaining the same end. Based on Johann Nestroy's *Einen Jux will es sich Machen,* a German adaptation of a 19th century English farce, John Oxenford's *A Day Well Spent,* the play might well be called the Complete Farce, centering on farce's basic concerns, folly, money and love, developing its story with complex and improbable plotting, filled with "screen scenes" involving sudden discoveries and disguises, and with characters brought on stage for the primary purpose of engineering the story to its close. Even in his use of typical 19th century stage costume, Wilder is trying to make his play a reproduction of an older style of dramaturgy. He succeeds so well that the play seems as good as any of its models; unfortunately, it seems no better. Old-style farce permits him to use cliché figures cleverly, and to stress the theatricalism which seems an essential part of his theatrical style. Yet in the empty trivialities of the story, the amorous escapades of the Merchant and his apprentices, Wilder deserts the long view of the human scene which justified the similar effects in *Our Town.* Farce, as farce always does, diminishes humanity, belittles the human scene, and commits itself only to the mechanics of laughter. *The Merchant of Yonkers,* even under the direction of the noted German producer, Max Reinhardt, failed when it was first produced. Engaging as it was, set against *Our Town* it meant little because its effects were produced for so little purpose.

The farcical theatricalism of *The Merchant of Yonkers* was combined with the more purposive antirealistic techniques in Wilder's next play, *The Skin of Our Teeth* (1942). *Our Town*'s stage manager is banished behind the wings, to be sure, but his anxious voice is heard in moments of production crisis, and his presence is felt everywhere. As in *Our Town,* the audience is continually reminded of itself by intrusive voices from the auditorium, by ushers participating in the destruction of the theater to "save the human race" from the Ice Age, and by the many kinds of free vaudeville which occur in the action. From backstage come dressers and stage hands to duplicate the passing of the planets and the hours, as in *Pullman Car Hiawatha,* and the swaying flimsiness of the scenery continually stresses the essentially illusory nature of the theatrical experience.

Added to this is the element of ancient theatrical farce, notably in Sabina's opening and closing soliloquy, where she is permitted to enact the part of the traditional comic maid delivering the exposition. The effect is to dispel illusion in a burlesque of antiquated stage conventions which emphasizes continually the theater's false face.

As in *Our Town* and, to a lesser extent, *The Merchant of Yonkers,* the devices minimize the particular psychology of the characters, turning them into figures in a charade who perform before a symbolic setting a deliberately unconvincing enactment of man's progress through the ages. Again, the temporal and spatial freedom permitted by the setting enables the action to move in fragmentary symbolic configurations forward and backward in time.

The Antrobus family is several specific families: it is the family unit of the cave-dwellers; it is Adam, Eve, Lilith; it is the family of Noah; it is the family of the average present-day suburban commuter. Its many specific identifications, however, combine to make it the archetype of all families in all times. It becomes "Every Family," the norm of the concept, much as the configurations in *Our Town* become norms. All images are blended in a composition of universal significance.

Thus far, Wilder develops what he has done before, holding his characters at a distance, that they may become symbols. But now, perhaps taking a hint from the stage manager's relations to his actors in *Pullman Car Hiawatha,* he also stresses that his actors are in fact actors, and he does with them what he had not done in *Our Town* or *The Merchant of Yonkers* — he gives them personal stories to enact within the larger frame of the drama.

The effect is a little like the infinity to be found in barbershop mirrors: Lilith, the eternal temptress, is a maid named Sabina, who is played by an actress named Miss Fairweather, who, in turn — once this aperture has been opened — was played by an actress named Tallulah Bankhead. Essentially a comic device, refined and put to more significant service than usual, the technique is similar to that which Shakespeare developed with his original Rosalind: a boy, pretending to be a girl, pretending to be a boy, pretending to be a girl, to the ultimate negation of any reality of character.

In Wilder's play, the device allows him to maintain the sense of comedy even when he portrays situations involving world cataclysm. Yet it is also true that this illumination behind the mask tends at certain points in the action to increase the audience's sense of identification with his characters at the same time that it maintains the long view. At its easiest level, the play has the delights of vaudeville. Thus, when Miss Bankhead read the line, "The Ten Commandments, faugh!" and added in a throaty aside what was evidently a deep personal conviction, "That's the worst line I ever had to say on any stage!" the Bankhead personality broke through layers of Fairweather and Sabina with an effect reminiscent of Hogarth's drawings of false perspective.

Not only serviceable for comic purposes, the device provides Wilder with the empassioned climax of his play. In Act III, when Cain's murderous frenzy becomes the actor's reality, when the artificial enactment of a symbolic gesture becomes the particular actor's truth, illusion and reality merge in a way that neither negates the effect of the passion nor permits the passion to come too close so as to destroy the essential perspective of the play. It is Wilder's particular ability to superimpose artifice on reality in this way, projecting life through his imagery.

In the end what Wilder achieves by his technical experiments with point of view and identification is freedom to depict man moving in great gaps of time, of the limited terrestrial animal who has a dim vision of eternity, and, because of it, somehow musters the will to survive.

After *The Skin of Our Teeth*, Wilder turned to matters other than the stage[2] until 1954, when his rewritten version of *The Merchant of Yonkers* opened under its new title, *The Matchmaker*. As directed by Sir Tyrone Guthrie, the play, no longer overshadowed by the success of *Our Town*, came into its own as an amiable piece of tomfoolery. The revisions are very slight, amounting in effect only to the kind of judicious pruning and tightening which any play may expect to undergo in production. At only one moment does Wilder make a significant alteration. Mrs. Levi's soliloquy at the end of Act IV which begins "Ephraim Levi, I'm going to get married again. . . ." contains in its original version a lengthy analysis of the people who refuse to accept the human race:

> You and I have known lots of people who've decided — like Horace Vangelder — not to live among human beings. Yes, they move about among them, they talk to them, they even marry them; but at heart they've decided not to have anything to do with the human race.
> They become secret.
> They ask nothing and they give nothing.
> They've refused the human race and perhaps they're right.
> And the first sign that a person's refused the human race is that he makes plans to improve and restrict the human race according to patterns of his own. It looks like love of the human race, but believe me, it's the refusal of the human race, — those blue-print worlds where everyone is supposed to be happy, and no one's allowed to be free.
> If you accept human beings and are willing to live among them, you acknowledge that every man has a right to his mistakes. . . .

The lines state clearly enough one of Wilder's creeds, and perhaps provide a partial explanation of his insistence that man is better off not knowing the nature of his destiny. Yet they are repetitious and overly

2 Omitted from consideration here are his early play, *The Trumpet Shall Sound* (1927), his translation of Andre Obey's *Lucrèce* which Katherine Cornell played in 1932, and his version of the Alcestis story, variously titled *The Alcestiad*, *The Drunken Sisters*, and *A Life in the Sun*. The latter was first staged at the Edinburgh Festival in 1955, but was withdrawn from the English stage thereafter. It has been published in German translation. Its first general appearance in English was as the libretto of an opera by Louise Talma. Wilder has been at work for some years on two cycles of one-act plays concerned with the Seven Deadly Sins and the Seven Ages of Man. When completed they are intended to be played in varying combinations over a series of evenings. Three of these plays were staged off-Broadway in 1962.

explicit, and in their sociological implications a little heavy for the tone of the farce.

In the revision, the lines are altered:

> After my husband's death I retired into myself. Yes, in the evenings, I'd put out the cat, and I'd lock the door, and I'd make myself a little rum toddy; and before I went to bed I'd say a little prayer, thanking God that I was independent — that no one else's life was mixed up with mine. And when ten o'clock sounded from Trinity Church tower, I fell off to sleep and I was a perfectly contented woman. And one night, after two years of this, an oak leaf fell out of my Bible. I had placed it there on the day my husband asked me to marry him; a perfectly good oak leaf — but without color and without life. And suddenly I realized that for a long time I had not shed one tear; nor had I been filled with the wonderful hope that something or other would turn out well. I saw that I was like that oak leaf, and on that night I decided to rejoin the human race.

The difference is partly in the tone, in the use of the concrete rather than the general, but mostly in the quality of the imagery. In its stress on growth and on the value of life, the imagery of this one speech is almost sufficient in itself to lift the farce from its emptiness, to turn it in the end to comedy.

Comedy should be distinguished from farce in two respects. First, it is not centrally satiric. Comic satire in drama always results in farce. In plays by Aristophanes, Ben Jonson, Molière, and Shaw, the generic form which their satire develops is that funny pattern of humanly improbable action where event is significantly separated from character. The work of Beckett and Ionesco has taught the playgoer once again that farce is capable of serious statement. As all drama can be, farce is a way of looking at life, and at times its particular distortions have no equal for reflecting an inherently distorted world. But farce in the hands of a great playwright is possessed by a demon. It is raised from a sterile existential hell and forced to caper insanely before laughing multitudes. In itself it generates no emotion. An audience for farce is a little like the farce itself — possessed by the attitudes of the playwright. The emotion is applied to the work, not developed within it. An audience is called to share Aristophanes' ribald rage and Molière's scorn but not primarily to understand or sympathize with the characters. What the characters mean is more important than what they do, because their every action only reiterates their hopelessness and their folly. With Ionesco, farce again antiseptically applies a styptic to emotion; with Beckett, although farce is often betrayed by sentimentalism, the end result is more likely to be a sense about Gogo, Didi, and Krapp than a feeling for them.

A second distinction between comedy and its grotesque counterpart follows from the first: that comedy is essentially positive and optimistic, whereas farce is negative in its view of the human condition. Its soulless comedians are generally not permitted any higher good than the merry and notable frauds of Aristophanes' Pisthetairos or Jonson's Volpone. Its world is the artificial construct of the cozener, tales told by a con man to deceive and delight. Whether the cheater be active for love, money, or both, in the end his actions ask no further commitment than that his audience share the dramatist's point of view toward the absurdity he has imaged onstage. The dramatist's truth is local and particular, framed in relationship to temporal criticism and manners, and his characters live, if at all, because folly persists, and in all times cheating is the immediate consequence of folly. Without these particular polarities, so essential in *The Matchmaker*, farce dies and is forgotten despite its wit, its structured cleverness, its frail memorials to the laughter of the dead.

But comedy is a testament to life. Its commitment is to the great regenerative cycle, following man's course from birth through nature to death. By no accident, comedy's main concern is often with love, courtship, and marriage. Comedy's laughter rises from the complications of wooing and of man's stumbling efforts to dominate the life process which grips him. In the great Shakespearean comedy, the laughter arises when the lovers for one reason or another pull away from nature, out of the cyclic process: when the girl destined for love disguises herself as a man, when a woman in obsessive mourning walls herself and her garden away from love. Such spinsters — Olivias, Violas, Rosalinds — and their masculine counterparts, the determined bachelors — the Berownes and Benedicks — as they separate from life, become guilty of folly and move, ironically enough, in the sterile patterns of farce. So Congreve's Mirabel and Millamant, before they "dwindle" into matrimony, move in a maze "like a dog in a dancing school." Yet nature and comedy make short work of the would-be farceurs, overwhelming them in the end and tossing them back to the living source of their blessing, to love, and its vital fulfillment.

It is truistic to acknowledge that in the twentieth century there has been no tragedy to compare with that of the Greek and Renaissance theaters. Often, the most serious criticism of both the contemporary theater and contemporary man is that they are incapable of tragic perception. Yet the point may equally well be made that there is today no comic perception either — a point which may suggest that unalloyed comedy and tragedy are alike in their central point of view and in their final assertion. Although comedy finds its fulfillment in life and tragedy its fulfillment in death, weddings and funerals celebrate the same natural process and both ceremonially testify to the value of the force and of the lives it controls.

For reasons apparent to any watcher of twentieth century skies, such unqualified testimony, such essentially religious testimony as tragedy and

comedy have traditionally offered cannot be easily found or readily accepted. The ceremonials which signify joining with or separating from
life bring little assurance of sanctity. Men marry and die in haste, and
comedy and tragedy have lost their affirmative assurance of life's lasting
fulfillments. Both have been hollowed out with farce and sentimentality
leaving the form of the thing without its essence, a partial and adulterate
perception lacking boldness and wisdom. At the best, a few dramatists
have sought after modern equivalents of the tragic and comic values in
mixed forms, which by their very impurity testify to the puzzling complexity of an irresolute, modern evaluation of life.

Thus far, in twentieth century American Drama, only two playwrights have proved durable beyond their season. In Eugene O'Neill,
there developed a tragedian of stature — awkward, gifted with a giant's
strength, sometimes guilty of using it like a giant, yet an artist who saw
with the clarity occasionally granted to the pessimist the way man's life
can be justified through suffering. At the same time, and conveying
something of the same sense of being a little out of the stream of the
main direction of American drama as O'Neill's work conveys, Thornton
Wilder wrote the three plays which have adhered most closely in this
country to the traditional vision and the affirmative concept of great
comedy.

In a foreword to *The Angel That Troubled the Waters,* Wilder
revealed clearly why this is so. He wrote:

> The art of literature springs from two curiosities, a curiosity about
> human beings pushed to such an extreme that it resembles love, and a love
> of a few masterpieces of literature so absorbing that it has all the richest
> elements of curiosity. I use the word *curiosity* in the French sense of a tire-
> less awareness of things. (It is too late to arrest the deterioration of our
> greatest English words. We live in an age where *pity* and *charity* have taken
> on the colors of condescensions; where *humility* is foolishness and *curiosity*
> is interference. Today *hope,* and *faith* itself, implies deliberate self-deception.

Wilder is right, of course. The sympathies which came so readily
and strongly to men in the past are now perplexing and adulterate, unable to abide questioning. Eugene O'Neill constructed an entire scheme
of tragedy on the hope that implies deliberate self-deception. Yet Wilder,
as his revision of Dolly Levi's soliloquy suggests, is not quite willing to
give over the polarities of past assurance: pity, charity, humility, simplicity, hope, faith, and the curiosity that leads to wonder. That he cannot deal with them as they essentially are but must cast them in terms
of cliché images from old theatrical modes is a consequence of the human
condition, not a necessary element in Wilder's faith. Of his first plays he
remarked that they are almost all religious plays, but, he added, "reli-

gious in that dilute fashion that is a believer's concession to a contemporary standard of good manners."

The concessions must be made. Perhaps, in dealing with religious themes in theatrical terms they have always to be made. Yet it is evident that the concessions are in the form of technical experimentations, of the way of presenting the themes, rather than in the themes themselves. At the center of his dramas, at least, Wilder makes no concession. That he does not explains much of his present pre-eminence and suggests why his work may survive the more ephemeral drama of his time.

joseph wood krutch

POSTWAR

With the exception of O'Neill, no playwright who contributed to the modern American drama wrote any important work before the outbreak of the First World War. Apparently, however, that was merely an accident of time and certainly the Second War did not mark the beginning of any distinct epoch. Inevitably, a certain number of war plays appeared, notably Robert Sherwood's *There Shall Be No Night* and Lillian Hellman's *Watch on the Rhine,* but these introduced neither a new writer nor a new aspect of his talent. And it is significant that the most popular war play, *Mister Roberts* by Thomas Heggen and Joshua Logan, was a sort of sea-going *What Price Glory,* reaffirming its ribald disrespect for the pride, pomp, and circumstance of glorious war which had made the earlier play unlike anything previous in our dramatic history. . . .

A number of writers whose reputations were already established continued to produce, and a few of them contributed plays worthy to be compared with their previous work. Maxwell Anderson's *Anne of the Thousand Days* was a historical verse drama more or less in the manner of *Elizabeth the Queen* and his *Joan of Lorraine* also utilized a historical theme; Odets's *The Big Knife* and *The Country Girl* reflected the author's new life as a Hollywood scenarist and though they attracted re-

Reprinted from *American Drama Since 1918,* George Braziller, Inc., 1957, © Joseph Wood Krutch.

newed attention to a writer with great theatrical talent neither had the strong individuality which first distinguished him. This seemed to have disappeared with the waning of his commitment to left-wing social convictions. Sidney Howard's entertaining fantasy on the Faust theme, *Madam, Will You Walk,* was written shortly before his death but did not reach New York until 1954. O'Neill provided two major new tragedies and George Kaufman continued his success in the old line with, among others, *The Man Who Came to Dinner,* written again in collaboration with Moss Hart. But perhaps the most original new twist to smart farce comedy was given by a new writer, Garson Kanin, whose enormously successful *Born Yesterday* tells the story of a seemingly "dumb blonde" who blossoms into social consciousness under the tutelage of a liberal journalist, turns the tables on her racketeer lover, and, reversing the old farce formula which traces the transformation of a Cinderella from glasses into glamor, traces her evolution from glamor to glasses.

In a more serious vein Thornton Wilder, previously known in the theater chiefly for *Our Town* which had been awarded the Pulitzer Prize in 1938, took that award again in 1943 for the very different *The Skin of Our Teeth* in which he uses what might be called the method of humorous surrealism to tell the whole history of civilization from the time of the cave man down to the present as though it had all happened to a certain Mr. Antrobus, his wife, and their siren-housemaid, Sabina (a veritable Lilith). Mr. Antrobus invents both the alphabet and the wheel and he survives "by the skin of his teeth" the Ice Age and a third world war — even though he is temperamentally incapable of seeing the calamities before they arrive and can never quite make up his mind how to choose between the mother of his children and the siren whose charms inspire him to conceive his happiest inventions. . . .

As for the short-story writer William Saroyan, his skyrocket rose so suddenly into the theatrical firmament and then fell from it so suddenly that he seems to belong, not to a decade, but to the single year 1939 which saw the production of the only two of his several plays to win enthusiastic praise from either reviewers or the general public. But both of these pyrotechnic displays were so original and delightful that they inspired reasonable hopes which the future did not fulfill though their author has continued more successfully as a writer of short stories and sketches.

Mr. Saroyan seemed to be everything uncharacteristic of a year which was just emerging from the gloom, anger, and dismay of the depression decade which had turned the thoughts of so many of his generation toward pessimism or, more often, revolutionary proposals to shatter our world to bits in order that it might be rebuilded nearer to what they supposed to be their hearts' desire. Mr. Saroyan was gay, exuberant, romantically an individualist, and so convinced that the world was full of "beautiful people" as well as of all manner of other delightful things that we should all be happy as kings if we would only relax, "breathe in and breathe out," and, as he also put it, "believe everything." Quick fancy, exuberant humor, a real gift for words, and occasional flashes of what were almost — sometimes perhaps actually — profound insights, all combined to produce an impression of astonishing freshness. The short-length *My Heart's in the Highlands,* told — by a technique halfway to expressionism — the story of a happy-go-lucky family which is completely converted to the Saroyanism it seems to have practiced all along by the appearance of a mysterious stranger who teaches philosophy by blowing "My Heart's in the Highlands" on a bugle. *The Time of Your Life,* full length and somewhat more conventional in structure, had as its ambiguous central character a mysterious youngish man of great, unexplained wealth who spends most of his time in a raffish saloon brooding over the problems of his existence and in various seemingly minor ways playing God to the beautiful people with whom he comes in contact. Various often delightfully eccentric persons float in and out but the hero's chief miracle is bringing to self-respect and a decent way of life a sad young prostitute with no love for her profession. Here Saroyan comes closer than before to unmistakable sentimentality but is saved by bubbling humor and unexpected moments of charming fancy. That none of his subsequent plays have quite come off or achieved theatrical success may be due in part to a simple exhaustion of the vein but is probably due also to an increasing slackness in construction, and what seems to be the failure to move in any discernible direction. Mr. Saroyan's theory that one should write by simply letting oneself go may have been responsible for the spontaneity of the first two plays but is more certainly responsible for the diffuse meanderings of the others.

O'Neill was unquestionably the most discussed playwright of the twenties and Odets of the thirties. During the decade just past the distinction has been shared almost equally by two newcomers neither of whom had been heard in the New York theater before 1945: Tennessee Williams whose first Broadway production, *The Glass Menagerie,* was given the Critics Prize for the season 1944–45 and Arthur Miller whose first, *All My Sons,* received the same award for 1946–47.

Mr. Miller's work is obviously related to that produced by the "socially conscious" playwrights of the thirties and also, rather more directly than the latter were, to the explicitly "social" plays of Ibsen. *All My Sons* was concerned with a dishonest manufacturer of war materials whose own son was killed because of a defect in one of the father's products. The play exhibited a talent sufficient to cause critics to overestimate somewhat its actual merits, which are diminished by a certain stiffness and a certain irony too simple, too neat, and obviously contrived. It exhibited also what has proved to be a characteristic hesitation on the part of the author in this important respect: he seems to want to imply, without quite explicitly committing himself to the implication, that this is not merely the story of an individual guilty man but that of an evil inevitably characteristic of "our social system." *Death of a Salesman,* his most successful and best play to date, tells the story of the final dismal years of a pathetic traveling salesman who is the victim partly of his own vulgar idea of success, partly of a social system which encourages just such vulgar ideals. Despite a few expressionistic touches the method is predominantly that of a literal, Dreiseresque naturalism, and the atmosphere is that of lives unrelievedly drab while the moral is again slightly ambiguous. . . .

The Crucible laid its scene at the time of the Salem witchcraft trials with the obvious intention of drawing a parallel between them and the "security trials" of the present day. Its validity depends upon the validity of the parallel and those who find it invalid point out that, whereas witchcraft was pure delusion, subversion is a reality, no matter how unwisely or intemperately it may be combatted.

The plays of Tennessee Williams, like those of Miller, are also what Shaw would have called "unpleasant plays." But in them the attention is centered persistently upon the inner life of the characters whose difficulties are presented as first of all psychological rather than social or political — whatever the relation between these psychological problems and the society in which they live may be. The stress is upon what is sometimes called "the irrational element" in human life and the central personages are neurotic rather than, as in Miller, the victims of false convictions and an evil social system. Unfavorable critics are likely to call Miller "doctrinaire" and "preachy"; Williams, "morbid."

He first attracted wide attention with *The Glass Menagerie* in which an absurd and pathetic widow who likes to think of herself as a member of the decayed Southern aristocracy, and hence the exponent of "gracious living," is not only disappointed in her efforts to find a husband for her shy, crippled daughter but is, in every other way, defeated by a crude and pushing modernity which neither understands nor respects her dream of gentility. *A Streetcar Named Desire,* perhaps his best play, again has as its theme a clash between an enfeebled tradition of gentility and a society which has never known what the term means. But in this play everything is heightened and pushed further in the direction of a morbid intensity. The heroine, Blanche DuBois, has broken under the strain and is torn between her ideal of gentility and a pathological impulse toward promiscuity, to the point where her sanity leaves her completely and she is led off to a madhouse. . . .

Inevitably comparisons are made between Miller and Williams on the one hand and O'Neill and Maxwell Anderson on the other. The two more recent writers are, like O'Neill and Anderson, men who achieved success with plays which can, loosely at least, be called "tragedies." In what sense are they all part of a continuing tradition? Can the works of Miller and Williams be called "true tragedies" or are they merely "unpleasant plays"?

Obviously neither Miller nor Williams plainly commits himself, as Anderson and O'Neill do, to either the form or content of classical tragedy. In his later short play, *A View from the Bridge,* Miller consciously seeks a link with classical tragedy. However, in their major plays neither he nor Williams exhibits as plainly as O'Neill a determination to seek persistently for something in the universe outside man to which he can appeal and "belong." Hence it is possible to interpret *Death of a Salesman* as brutal naturalism and *A Streetcar Named Desire* as a sort of semi-surrealist version of the Strindbergian submission to destructive obsessions. Alternately, both might perhaps be interpreted as, in a loose sense, "existentialist." . . .

Seen in [another] light Miller is a moralist in very much the same sense that Ibsen was a moralist, and the play [*Death of a Salesman*] becomes a qualified reaffirmation of the individual's privilege of being, within certain limits, what he chooses to be.

The case of Williams is different but equally dubious. The most obvious interpretations put him among the despairing explorers of pathological states of mind just as the obvious interpretations put Miller among the sociological naturalists. In Williams's two most striking plays the central character is obsessed; and in *A Streetcar Named Desire* the obsession takes a sexual form. But in both there is another theme. Each of the heroines includes among her obsessions the fact that she is, or was, "a lady." In both the ideal of respectability, the sense that her parents and her remoter ancestors lived in accord with some code to which she herself would like to be loyal if she could, is so strong as to appear of crucial importance. In *The Glass Menagerie* the mother sees her family disintegrating because it no longer finds her dream of gentility more than annoying. In *A Streetcar Named Desire* the heroine seems to succumb to crude sexuality because she so fanatically refused to accept a normal life among people who appear to her as hopelessly unrefined. . . .

In any case the plays of Miller and Williams were major events in a decade of the American drama and would be the only major events had it not been for the appearance in 1956 of O'Neill's posthumous *Long*

Day's Journey Into Night which unexpectedly reaffirmed his greatness.

None of the three works by O'Neill to appear after the war could be said to have done quite that. *The Iceman Cometh,* though impressive, seemed to surrender to a nihilistic pessimism which destroyed the tension of his best plays by abandoning the struggle against utter hopelessness. Neither *A Moon for the Misbegotten* nor *A Touch of the Poet* (neither of which reached Broadway) revealed any new aspect of his talent or achieved an expression of it equal to that in his best previous work. In fact, O'Neill threatened to retreat into the past. Critics were sometimes saying that he had been overestimated; the few revivals of his work were not very successful; and there was some tendency to regard him as only "historically important." But *Long Day's Journey Into Night* is certain to encourage re-examination and an upward reassessment.

Frankly autobiographical, the great length is justified by the effect of solidity which the length makes possible. The names given to the characters are not their real names but there is no attempt to disguise anything and the play frankly presents the real persons and the relationship between them as they appeared to O'Neill himself. . . .

With the minor exception of the comedy *Ah, Wilderness!,* none of O'Neill's other successful plays is so purely domestic or remains so consistently upon the level of the merely literal and rational without even a suggestion of symbolism. Yet the remarkable fact is that without transcending the limits of domestic drama it manages to involve by implication the large themes with which O'Neill has always been concerned.

Since the play is so frankly autobiographical it would have considerable interest if it were no more than a confession and even if it were inferior as drama. But it is so far from being inferior as drama that it would be powerful and absorbing if there were no known connection between it and the actual events of the author's life. It would still raise as it does those unanswerable questions which lie at the heart of drama.

Two such questions are here linked together and the first is the question of a human being's responsibility for his own character and fate. The family involved was as doomed as any generation of the house of Atreus. But to what extent is that doom self-imposed?

Each member is determined to exculpate himself, to lay the blame elsewhere. The mother blames the father for the parsimony and irresponsibility which have driven her to drugs. The wastrel brother blames both for having given him no example and no home. The poet-to-be blames them for all this plus the neglect of his illness which has driven him to despair. But is it or is it not still true that, despite this welter of exculpation and blame, each is in his own way guilty because he has used the character and the actions of the others as an excuse for his own failures? Why does one son succumb to circumstances and the other triumph over them? Is the fault in the stars or in ourselves that we are thus and so?

The second fundamental question is posed in the case of the hero alone. He is telling us very frankly the outward and very special reasons which might be said to account for the sombreness of his view of human life. Does this mean, as some psychologists would maintain, that this explains or explains away his philosophy? It is, so they would say, only a rationalization and generalization of his own experience. To them what appears to be the tragic sense of life expressed in his plays is "nothing but" the maladjustment produced by a singularly unhappy childhood and youth. To them O'Neill was a man understandably but merely sick, one whose morbid fancies may be easily dismissed by those who are "normal" and "adjusted."

But thus we may attempt to explain away not only O'Neill but all writers who have had a tragic view of life. Is the conclusion really justified? All men have had experiences of one sort or another which have influenced them. But are their thoughts, and feelings, and beliefs "nothing but" these influences? Are their conclusions "nothing but" a rationalization? Or are they instead general truths which individual experience has enabled them to discover? Do O'Neill's plays really mean nothing except that he happened to have an unhappy childhood and youth? Or is there really, as O'Neill believed, a heart of darkness within the human soul which some are led to discover and some are not?

These two great questions, the question of human responsibility for what is called Fate and the question of what general truth the tragic situation illustrates, are perhaps the questions which true tragedy always raises. A play which raises them so urgently, while at the same time telling a powerful, convincing, and absorbing story is a major contribution to our dramatic literature.

laurence kitchin

THE POTENT INTRUDER
AMERICAN DRAMA AND ITS INFLUENCE

In August 1959, at the miniature British Drama League theatre in Fitzroy Square, Odets's *Waiting for Lefty* was given two performances under the direction of Charles Marowitz. Sitting next to me was a West End theatrical agent, there to spot talent. The play opens with an irruption of actors into the audience through the pass door, talking loudly, as if they were assembling for a trade-union meeting. When these came in, the agent mistook them for members of the public and indignantly told them to keep quiet. His mistake helped me to reconstruct the impact this play about a New York strike of taxi drivers must have made in 1935, when the Group Theatre first performed it, and also to recapture the thrill aroused by their *Golden Boy* at the St. James's in 1938.

Yet we are now so far from the strenuous political feelings of the thirties that strikes arise from abstruse grievances too trivial to engage the sympathy of those not involved, votes are cast with an eye to luxuries unexpected by the proletariat of those days. Arnold Wesker has already looked back, in *Chicken Soup with Barley*, with indulgence on the generation which was passionate about politics, and Marowitz was careful to describe *Waiting for Lefty* in his programme as a period piece. But on that August evening it still came across with the impact of anger rooted in hunger and the instinct of self-preservation. Heckling from the infiltrators among the audience and the speech of the trade-unionist on the stage conveyed a brutal, sinewy vigour which had survived twenty-four years of political upheaval since the original performance. The declension from this to the exhibitionist hero of William Inge's *Picnic*, in conflict with a desperate schoolmistress whose advances he has repulsed, is steep and depressing; like the decline of the American musical from *Oklahoma*, which celebrates the superiority of the farmer to the cowboy, down to *West Side Story*, a gangster version of *Romeo and Juliet* drawing more of its vitality from violence than from love.

Sentimentality and violence, opposite sides of the same debased

From *Mid-Century Drama* by Laurence Kitchin. Copyright © by Laurence Kitchin, 1960. Reprinted by permission of Faber and Faber Ltd.

coin, are now on the increase in American drama[1] to a degree that reflects favourably on the new English playwrights, deeply indebted though many of them are to American models. To my mind Arthur Miller was mistaken in having one man forcibly kiss another in *A View from the Bridge*, just as Pinero was wrong to let one of his heroines throw a Bible in the fire. In both cases the appeal is not of the kind a dramatist wants to exert on an audience when he is at the top of his form. The type of person who reacts strongly to such incidents is unlikely to appreciate anything less frivolous the play may be trying to communicate, while the others will at once be on the watch for a failure of inspiration. It is nothing to do with morality, simply a matter of right and wrong ways of putting an audience on the alert. Although it contains material of great sociological interest I was quite unable to take *Tea and Sympathy* seriously, because it ended with a teacher's wife seducing one of her husband's pupils. If the comic aspect of an episode like that is not to dominate all others, it should occur while there is still time to quell the ribald associations aroused.

The raping of Blanche du Bois by Stanley Kowalski in *A Streetcar Named Desire* is in the same class of sensationalism, because it occurs after the theme of the play and its central character have been fully explored. It brings us down abruptly to the level of pulp fiction. So does the prominence of the bed in the setting of *Cat on a Hot Tin Roof*. As Tennessee Williams is careful to point out in his notes to the designer, it should be slightly raked so that people on it can be better seen. Like his finicky stage directions about details of female dress and its accessories, these examples illustrate an aspect of Williams as a playwright which suits the taste of a consumer society content that its films and television programmes should be mostly directed at a feminine audience. But the foreground of dramatic action can absorb only a limited degree of sensationalism without loss of total impact; what was hailed as the century of the common man has become in mid-course the century of the common woman and the playwright is faced with new dangers as well as new subjects.

In American drama the surface agitation we have already noticed in contemporary revivals of the classics now tends to obscure deeper conflicts which are the backbone of O'Neill, Miller and the early Odets. What could be simpler than the dramatic axis of *Golden Boy*: a young man whose hands can both box and play the violin? Once you have granted that unlikely premise, the personal tensions crystallize neatly and something about conflicting ways of life can be said. The framework will carry a great deal of personal emotion, including the refinements of

---

[1] ". . . most playwrights are devoted to dramatizing situations which grow more hysterical and rarefied with every passing year." Robert Brustein in *Harper's Magazine*, October, 1959.

Method acting, as Morris Carnovsky and Luther Adler proved at the St. James's, with little danger of the actors swamping the play. What could be bolder than the notion, in *Waiting for Lefty* of turning the stage into a trade-union platform and the audience into involved participants? The device automatically produces involvement of some sort, like the question: "Who are you neutral against?", said to have been hurled by an Irish brawler at spectators on the sidelines. And what could be richer, in contemporary terms of social and moral conflict, than Miller's idea in *All My Sons* of having a manufacturer fit up an entire squadron with defective engines, then wash his hands of the consequences because the cylinder caps *might* have got by, and, anyway, he didn't happen to know the fliers personally? In all these cases the playwright has firmly decided what is to be the centre of gravity, has raised his work above the caprices of directors and future audiences, laid down conditions from which everything else will flow. Whereas in *A Hatful of Rain,* admittedly built as a showcase for Method acting, the interest is in the parade of junky symptoms. In *Orpheus Descending, The Rose Tattoo, Picnic* and *The Rainmaker* the decline in creative control is a lesser one, but perceptible. All four stem from a sexual catalyst, dropped into the stagnant water of a torpid community. The construction depends on a formula which cannot fail to produce action of a kind, any more than it can avoid novelet-tish appeal to fantasies of wish-fulfilment such as cling to the ending of *Tea and Sympathy.*

It is a matter of some urgency to make these discriminations, because American drama springs from the society which sets the pattern of life in mid-century England, and is diffused by television and the cinema as well as the theatre. From the social point of view it elucidates our own behaviour and may even determine it. Moreover, it has been ahead of ours for two decades in social criticism, psychology, animal spirits, in all the elements, except acting and classical revivals, which go to make up a mature dramatic art. The London commercial theatre, smugly rooted in economic opportunism, weakened its defences against the new English mid-century drama by letting in on an American ticket work which is radically subversive. Political and sexual taboos were lifted to admit Miller and Williams. Precedent after precedent was established, until the new native drama was able to swim into the West End over obstructive groynes on a high tide. Since few people now in their twenties could have seen any vital new plays not of American, or now and then French origin, it is surprising how quickly some of them, including Shelagh Delaney and Arnold Wesker, have developed an English accent.

For practical purposes American drama has won a place in the European tradition and the playwright's license to draw on it sensibly is inescapable. The fact that it is, at any rate temporarily, in decline, need not obscure the achievements, of which the most fruitful has been of special relevance to the public art of drama, a genius for *keeping in touch*. First Odets was in touch as a dramatist with the pragmatic thirties, then Miller with the economics of hot war and the fanaticism of cold war. Now Williams, in touch with the primitive urges of half-educated people maladjusted to prosperity, reflects Subtopia and the Beat generation; while O'Neill, posthumously at that, is crowned laureate of the tranquillizer, the romantic dreamer's escape from stimuli too spicy for his digestion.

Meanwhile, in England, many laid their bets on the revival of verse drama initiated by T. S. Eliot and carried on by Christopher Fry. It built up a respectable circulation in cathedrals and training colleges, but has remained obstinately on the margin of public taste in spite of eminent sponsorship. One reason is that the movement was closely related from the start to ecclesiastical policy, for two decades in which churchgoers were a very small minority. It also suffered from an academic approach to theatrical form, and the assumption, common to a similar movement in America, that the next significant advance would come as an act of grace by the literary establishment, from above, instead of, as actually happened on both sides of the Atlantic, from the working classes. The initial indignation aroused by John Osborne reflected the jolt he had given to that assumption. How seriously the "poetic revival" was out of touch was clear at the time in Fry's *The Lady's Not For Burning* (1948). Not only was the title and much of the tone lacking in tact at a time of ruthless persecution, but the verbal arabesques, at play above the vacuum where a dramatic situation could have been, were proofs that a promising subject was in the wrong hands. Miller's *The Crucible*, in touch with both contemporary and historical issues latent in the same subject, gave it an artistically richer treatment in plainer words. As in *Waiting for Lefty*, the action would have lost focus if an author's verbal dexterity had been in the foreground. Nobody wants to read a murder trial or a declaration of war in elaborately allusive language.

The spate of imitators in three different media tends to obscure the outlines of Miller's place in the scheme. Hence the necessity to define it again. There is the working-class childhood, the professional education in the drama department of the University of Michigan, and there is the Marxism, controversial, of course, which backs his work with the authority of an intellectual tradition, as well as leading him to points of collision between contradictory claims, between conformity and self-expression, conscience and the profit motive. These qualifications might add up to no more than a blueprint for committed drama of the kind eroded by every change in the political climate, were it not for Miller's ability to perform the initial act of selection so many others evade. He goes in with a scalpel, dissects the morally diseased tissue at the roots of his theme and describes in human terms the damage it does to the body as a whole. There is a parade, not of symptoms but of people exhibiting symptoms, and there is no gloating, nothing like the persecution Williams inflicts on Brick, Blanche and Big Daddy. Everything depends on the kind of relationship Ibsen establishes in *An Enemy of the People* — of which, incidentally, Miller has done an adaptation — between various forms of vested interest and the challenging fact of a polluted sewer. In Miller's plays the direct source of corruption is a specific human weakness: Loman's insistence, disastrous in its effect all round, on being "well liked", Keller's on pushing family ambitions to an anti-social extreme which even his own son can't accept.

Just as, in Ibsen, Rosmer's weakness turns out unexpectedly to have been the main structural support of the play, because it is plausible, representative, incurable and not wholly unsympathetic, so Miller builds firmly on rifts in the social fabric. Compared with others, four acts of brutally expressive façade enclosing a void, his plays put one in mind of contemporary architecture when it relies for stability on central pillars unseen from outside. Confidence increases the further you penetrate, for Miller has a particle of Ibsen's gift, which Shaw never understood, in peeling away the more rigidly political implications of a subject until we are dealing with human problems no longer limited by the original social context. *All My Sons*, which seems for a time to be developing on the lines of a denunciation of war profiteers, justifies its title by coming out with an attitude, difficult to separate from the Christian one, in favour of extending love and protection beyond the limits of the family. The action of great drama has always been in this sense interior, and a parallel would be with Ibsen's gradual dismissal of its political line-up to the background of *Rosmersholm*.

Having seen Frederick March on the cinema, Albert Dekker on television, but not Muni on the stage, in *Death of a Salesman*, I cannot tell how far the 'turbulent longings' demanded in the stage directions could be acted in such a way as to bring Willy Loman nearer to King Lear and further from Zero, the central figure in Elmer Rice's *The Adding Machine*. Loman, an ageing drummer, is licked from the start and not helped out by anything like the self-assertion O'Neill allows Hickey, his counterpart in *The Iceman Cometh*, before he crumbles. Although this time he seems to have let his diagnosis of weakness weaken the dramatic effect, it may be mere pedantry to fault Miller because he fails to give Loman tragic stature. What has tragedy to do with Subtopia? Perhaps the whole point is that Loman, the main support of the action, is horribly disintegrating before our eyes. His brother Ben, "the only man I ever met who knew the answers", had to deal with an altogether different set of questions, and Loman, as one of his sons remarks at the funeral, "never knew who he was". Lear did.

The limited degree of insight available to such a character, pitiably condition, as his creator recognizes, by commercial pressures, is a handicap not only in this play but through the whole range of American drama and of the new English drama as well. I have often suspected that Shaw, so very articulate, was ill at ease in landing himself in *Saint Joan* with the equivalent of an uneducated spiritualistic medium as his heroine; the part lapses badly into dialect and pseudo-poetry. The interest is not in her personally, nor Miller's in Loman. At one point his wife has to say: "He's not the finest character that ever lived. But he's a human being, and a terrible thing is happening to him. So attention must be paid." She calls twice more for attention, and it sounds like the appeal a dramatist makes to the audience when he's not quite sure they are with him. Both plays have an epilogue, of course, always something of a letdown because it is in the nature of theatre audiences to resent anything which abrubtly destroys continuity and has the flavour of an afterthought. Resolution, following at once on a climax, taps deeper sources of response.

With these reservations, *Death of a Salesman* (1948) is a masterpiece of concentrated irony and controlled indignation. One of Loman's sons throws his father's ethos away after a protracted struggle; the other pursues it in a more corrupt form. Biff, the recalcitrant one, draws his rebellion in Miller's best manner, more from disgust at one of his father's infidelities than from any reasoned objection to what he has been taught. Nothing short of a slur on that universal idol, the American's mother, could have roused this character from his mental lethargy, and a suitable occasion is provided. The idol herself learns nothing; we leave her puzzled because her hubsand chose to kill himself at a time when they were free from mortgage and hire-purchase obligations for the first time in thirty-five years. Her other son has "an apartment, a car, and plenty of women. And still, goddamnit, I'm lonely." All this when Bernard, the neighbour whom Loman has taught his sons to despise and who may be a projection of the author, is a happily married executive. Then again, Biff is well suited to life as a cowboy on twenty-eight dollars a week and only resents it when home influence taunts him with failure. The ironies intercross in scene after scene, always in the sense that there exists a mature solution for the problems but that none of this family knows what it is. Loman has seen to that, by transmitting to his sons only the narcissism of a salesman, a target of dollars, and success fantasies born of increasing disgust with his own servitude. Now old age, fatigue, obsolescence and the backwash of his mistakes are brought to bear on him ruthlessly. It would be an ugly sight if Miller were not dissecting a sick society rather than one man.

Altogether the texture of this play, although the lines are austerely naturalistic and the surface action frequently explosive, is of a close-grained allusiveness not to be found in minor works of art. Some of Biff's actions take one straight to known sources of juvenile delinquency; numerous episodes seem to bear out Reisman's sociological findings in *The Lonely Crowd,* and so on. Add this to the constructive ability and moral preoccupations already referred to, which invite some comparison with a master like Ibsen, and the conclusion must be that Miller is a dramatist from whom all others now living could learn something to their advantage.

Fortunately the new English drama shows many traces of his influence, most of which can be inferred from the above analysis by anyone who cares to consult, say, *Flowering Cherry* or *The Entertainer.* To list them in detail would need a book. But one further point about *Death of a Salesman* has to be raised: its scarifying relevance to English life in the year 1960. The ritual washing of the family car, the instalments on the washing machine, "Do it Yourself", the record album of children's prattle compiled by their proud father, the cliché "personality wins the day" which lies behind so much television programme planning, the hope that the mediocre Biff may be a late developer "like Thomas Edison" — by all his carefully selected social debris Miller demonstrates the drift away from values which help a man to know who he is. It is precisely the drift against which the new English drama has to struggle, and a decade later the environment here is the same. Loman, hemmed in by cars and apartment houses, no longer enjoys the urban slave's atavistic escape to his own gardening. He says: "They massacred the neighbourhood." In Reisman's jargon, inner-direction has given way to other-direction. Suburbia has become Subtopia.

Nothing I have yet been able to discover in the plays of Tennessee Williams comes up to Miller's combination of social perceptiveness and organically rich dramatic construction. One is always suspicious of an author who repeatedly drives criticism back to defend him in terms of his 'sense of the theatre' or of how much better the American production was; and, in any case, reference to the film versions can rectify many injustices done by faulty interpretation, just as reference to the printed text, especially the flatulent prefaces, tends to confirm defects obvious on the stage. The fact is that Williams is more representative than Miller of mid-twentieth-century taste, as we have seen it coming into focus during our examination of classical acting. Compared with Odets and Miller, who must seem to many of them as remote from their concerns as the Bostonian novels of John P. Marquand, Williams speaks to the young in a more sympathetic dramatic idiom. He deals, for example, in the shock of recognition — two shocks for the price of one in *Cat*, when Brick exchanges a diagnosis of cancer for Big Daddy's diagnosis of homosexuality. Williams is also concerned with every nook and cranny of the immediate stage effect, with lighting, costume and music, insisting in the production notes to *Summer and Smoke* that "colour harmonies and other visual effects are tremendously important". One result is that his plays never bore one at a first visit. The stage is alive in the sense that something vigorously expressive is always going on somewhere, if not on the cyclorama, then in the dialogue, and if not there, perhaps in some prop like Blanche's paper lantern or in a snatch of song.

This resembles the way tachiste and action painters animate a canvas with incontrovertible proof of artistic activity. Bursting on the chatty naturalism of the West End commercial theatre's postwar routine, Williams reminded a new generation of many almost forgotten things the theatre is for. He bombards the senses in such a way that attention must be paid; he doesn't ask for it, he grabs it. And these profuse strains of premeditated art are nothing if not expressive. Expressive of what? With that question, which has to be asked, the critic is at once in danger of being called a square, and when that happens his usefulness to the public art of drama is reduced, for he will be assumed to have opted out of the creative energy of his time. In evaluating Williams he will reveal how he is likely to respond to the new English drama, which, apart from direct imitation, draws on the same neo-romantic assumptions, the same cult of primitivism, exoticism and violence. Three considerations, however, lessen the critic's risk of creating a chasm between himself and his readers instead of a bridge. Whereas Williams is in his forties and seems to be maturing less noticably than Anouilh, with whom he has something in common, his imitators are in an early stage of development, still in a position to pick and choose. Secondly, the best of them are, in my opinion, sounder in their dramatic approach to human relationships already. Thirdly, their attention is increasingly drawn to the Romantic Movement itself, and there is no need to freeze one's responses to that at the level of Mrs. Radcliffe, early Keats and Fuseli.

Drama is about people, and the most humane aspect of Williams as a dramatist is his determination to speak up for the emotionally underprivileged. "Oh," says Alma in *Summer and Smoke*, "I suppose I am sick, one of those weak and divided people who slip like shadows among you solid strong ones. But sometimes, out of necessity, we shadowy people take on a strength of our own." It is a kind of strength very difficult to render in theatrical terms and perhaps only Chekhov has yet found an acceptable way. Vershinin, of course, is a classic example of the sexual catalyst who justifies the chemical analogy by remaining virtually unchanged himself after the stir he has caused in a backwater. The Moscow Art Theatre now render Lopakhin as if he, too, had something of this function. One sees how useful the formula is, for shadowy people fall below the minimum degree of outline stage characters normally require if their conflict is to hold an audience. The potent intruder can give them definition in relation to each other and to him. You find him, where the rest of the characters are not shadowy but merely conventional or out of stock, in work as different in other respects as *Amphitryon* 38 and *The Passing of the Third Floor Back*.

The use Williams makes of this formula gives a fair indication of the way in which he has developed from the twilit quietism of his earlier pieces towards an increasing sensationalism. In *The Glass Menagerie* the intruder is treated on the lines suggested by his suburban status as a "gentleman caller", while in *The Rose Tattoo* he has coarsened into the clownish truck driver who drops a contraceptive on the floor, just as the genteel earlier heroines have given way to strident Serafina, boasting of her late husband's virility. Although there is no longer anything shadowy about either of these contestants, the dust they raise is so blinding that we find it difficult to decide whom or what we are asked to be neutral against. They give us, not the Odets feeling of being caught in a street fight, but the more detached one of overhearing some domestic squabble in a tenement. There has been a gain in turbulence, with less impact than comes from a collision of rival causes.

What is being expressed? What is all the fuss about? In a *coup de théâtre*, Serafina smashes to pieces the vase containing her late husband's ashes, but that only tells us she is now ready for another man. Yet Lea Padovani's magnificently realistic performance in London pointed towards a more interesting statement, towards a creature of abounding vitality running to seed because of primitive Catholicism misapplied ("To me the big bed was beautiful like a religion"). If this is the theme, her scene with the local priest misses a chance to focus it and peters out in Serafina's contempt for local society; and if that is the theme it is sketched, not realized. The suspicion is that Williams is overwhelmed by his own creation and not in control. Instead of enrichments the ambiguities are a distraction, born of episodic profusion which lacks the shape an initial act of selection by the playwright would impose. Are we, for instance, to believe Serafina's claims for her husband? Padovani delivered them rather as one scoring a point against two silly women who accuse her of envying their success with men. You had no obligation to take the claims literally, but the text wants them to be made "suddenly and religiously".

Alvaro, the catalyst truck driver, is given here as much as he can handle in the way of dramatic resistance and the hero of *Orpheus Descending* too much. Foreshadowed by the postscript use of the device in

Summer and Smoke, where Alma picks up a stranger in the park, their loss of face corresponds to a steady increase in rampant femininity, from *The Rose Tattoo* to *Cat.* While the atmosphere of neurosis and sexual privation thickens, it becomes less and less helpful to approach these plays as the investigations of loneliness they are often held to be. The characters are, it is true, lonely people, in the sense of being cut off by repressed instincts clamouring for discharge. They drug themselves with superstition (Serafina) or alcohol (Brick), yet are scarcely shown to be suffering from anything which the appropriate tussle in bed cannot cure. Such predicaments, however robust and complicated the surrounding action may be, bring them closer to the persecuted college boy in *Tea and Sympathy* and his casual mate than to the conscious loneliness of Chekhov's people. Too many human factors are left out, and though Williams relates his characters to the wider social context that affects us all, he tends to make it romantically atmospheric, like the flower-seller in *Streetcar.* How well he could work in another direction he shows in the cash-nexus aspect of *Cat,* which yields more mature results than his melodramatic use of Brick's crutch and the bed. In a different way Pinero can offer the same frustrating mixture of insight and gimmick. But *Cat* leaves us in fatal doubt as to the author's valuation of what takes place. Maggie, the deprived wife, triumphantly asserts her marital rights at last, in reward for the energy and intelligence we have admired throughout. Our assent to her success remains naggingly modified by suspicion of her motives, which seem to include a mercenary greed as repulsive as anything her opponents exhibit. Based on experience of poverty, it is greed rooted in fear and would repay much exploration. This problem is never resolved. Instead our attention is occupied, or diverted, by the jubilant ending of her sexual drought.

In *Cat,* Williams at least got clear of the catalyst formula and shadowy people, the last of whom — Blanche in *Streetcar* — is explored very thoroughly, then lingeringly blotted out. Working in an opposite direction from the former one, the playwright here brings the shadow to the substance. Now it is the shadow of personality stretched to breaking point between gentility and nyphomania, the substance of Stanley's mating call, a popular equivalent of Olivier's howl in *Oedipus.* Although *Streetcar* succeeds in transmitting a *frisson* of one kind or another from start to finish, the sensationalism which invades Williams's later work strikes here very crudely on too vulnerable a victim. The real crisis comes when Blanche confesses her nymphomaniac exploits to Mich, the timid wooer who is her last hope, and he rejects her. After that, there is the dramatically false crisis of Stanley's assault on her, followed by the sadistic episode of her dismissal to a mental home. If Stanley were to be anything more than the most dangerous of many factors working against

Blanche's pretensions, then he deserved an opponent nearer his own fighting weight: Serafina or Maggie the Cat. The playwright's exchange of a rose-tinted microscope for a battering ram, at this point in what ought to have been the resolution of *Streetcar,* reflects in one play the decline traceable since in American drama as a whole. Stage violence, except perhaps at the box office, is subject to a law of diminishing returns.

No amount of emotional power, expressiveness in mood and atmosphere, sense of the theatre and eye for the arresting conflict can reach major drama if, as seems to me the case with Tennessee Williams, there is uncertainty or perversity in the handling of human relationships. That is why, though you automatically refer to Ibsen during a discussion of Miller, it is Pinero who comes to mind in relation to Williams. Extended comparison of *His House in Order* with *Cat* might be revealing in more ways than one, but a deeper affinity lies in comic talent very much underrated. To me Blanche du Bois is even more of a comic figure than the wife in *Tea and Sympathy,* with the very big difference that something in the attitude of Blanche's creator connives at such a view. After all, he gives her unlimited supplies of the self-deception and social pretension which lend themselves to a comic purpose. Perhaps that is why *Streetcar,* with its perversely Strindbergian ending, looms in the memory like a monstrous offspring of *The Father* and *Portrait of a Lady.* And comedy is demonstrably within Williams's range. Amanda, the mother in *The Glass Menagerie,* is extremely funny, the author who makes her speak of "the handwriting on the wall" an expert in conscious bathos. This talent is on the prowl later in *Cat* and *The Rose Tattoo,* insufficiently nourished. What I believe to be its proper function as a solvent in the lush fertility has been usurped by booster injections of emotion and by an intellect not up to the job.

As we are dealing with a major influence, if not *the* major influence on contemporary English drama, time may have been saved by following Williams to the dead end he seems to have reached. For a decade he has, in fact, occupied the place in theatrical history staked out for itself by the abortive poetic revival. The result is that a new generation of theatregoers take it for granted that the stage should vibrate with light and busy action, that metrical skill is no substitute for a strong situation, that dialogue is fluent prose enriched by colloquialisms and that poverty is a mine of local colour. All these, except perhaps the last neo-romantic assumption, represent an advance on the tired commercial drama. The exception is revealing, for where the problems treated in *Waiting for Lefty* and *Death of a Salesman* are closely concerned with economic survival and work, the characters in plays by Williams are at grips with an overriding mid-century problem: leisure. They are face to face with themselves and the U. S. A. Since their creator, who has expressed a preference for the Hemingway of *The Sun Also Rises,* has neither the Odets-Miller Marxist discipline nor O'Neill's Freudian solutions to offer them, but only a vague admiration for D. H. Lawrence, is it any wonder that they find each other difficult to live with? Proletarian drama in an era of prosperity drops easily into picture-postcard romanticism or toothless quarrels between the half-educated and the unteachable.

This may account for the surprisingly warm welcome given to late O'Neill when *The Iceman Cometh,* brilliantly directed by Peter Wood, was put on at the Arts in 1958. Here was the old master of neo-romanticism, who had used the ballad "Shenandoah" in counterpoint to Puritan guilt in *Mourning Becomes Electra* a quarter of a century before, introduced Captain Brand as a sexual catalyst in the same play, anticipated Stanley Kowalski in *The Hairy Ape,* run the entire post-war course of stage neurosis with precise Freudian accuracy, squeezed "African" local colour till the pips fell out in *The Emperor Jones* and found, in recent history, a suitable soil for Greek tragedy, which is more than Cocteau ever did. And now O'Neill was exploiting the drugged inertia sensationalism takes refuge in as the only alternative to its rioting luxuriance. Younger playgoers at once pronounced his Skid Row alcoholics authentic; they had seen them in *On the Bowery* on the pictures.

The Iceman Cometh is an old man's play, colourless, defeatist, written in the no longer fashionable naturalistic convention about social outcasts who have opted out of reality. Why did it appeal to the imagination of a gifted young director and gain instant success with an alert minority of mid-century theatre-goers? The answer seems to be that all audiences, including the television audience which responds well to Ibsen, develop a craving for dramatic experience organized in depth every bit as insistent as their more obvious craving for surface colour. It is wrong to assume, as commercial interests and creative theatre groups equally do, that any one line of approach to the public can be relied on. Something like late O'Neill or *Waiting for Godot* appears. Then everyone wonders why it takes on, although there is cool jazz as well as hot, the black and white violence of Swedish films alongside Hollywood scarlet, not only Turner but Caspar Friedrich catching all eyes at the Romantic Movement exhibition.

Close to proletarian drama in subject, though not in treatment, *The Iceman Cometh* is a major work which sums up the American achievement and offers a technical standard for the new English playwrights to keep in mind, although O'Neill's pessimism is in the end a crippling subjective limitation which, happily, this young movement rejects. New Orleans local colour and Sicilian squabbles are healthier imaginative diet in the early stages of growth.[2] Drawn to *The Iceman Cometh* by its documentary authority and the topical relevance of Hickey to the salesman installed by television in their homes, young addicts of drama may still become curious about the play's fascinating use of apparently drab material. Isolate some of the elements in its construction, and we indicate the important place systematic planning can have in the impact of mature drama. . . .

Apart from the astonishing narrative skill which brings first one and then another of a crowd of sluggish deadbeats into prominence and keeps up the hypnotic motion of creatures in an aquarium tank, O'Neill draws on a modification of the potent intruder formula. Hickey, the salesman who sells the alcoholics a cure which turns out to be worse than the disease, derives from Gregers Werle in *The Wild Duck*, alludes pungently to the wider social context of which Miller is the spokesman, and goes one better by relating its attitudes to those of evangelical religion. Ian Bannen's unctuously glib rendering of this part in the Arts Theatre production reminded me forcibly of Dr. Billy Graham's expert use of mass-media technique on his congregation at Harringay Arena.

Hickey, it turns out, is sucked deeper into the despair he seems to conflict with than any of the others. Such irony has no bottom; but Hickey's behaviour, on which the entire action of *The Iceman Cometh* arches steadily to a climax, is only one of two major themes. The other is the relationship between Larry, the lapsed syndicalist-anarchist, and Parritt, the renegade who has betrayed his own mother and wants to transfer the guilt. Hickey's arrest, which disposes of one theme, is closely followed by Parritt's suicide, which resolves the other. Larry is in conflict with both Hickey and Parritt throughout, so that the two knockout blows are delivered in harmony. In addition, Larry is an educated man. He still retains enough reasoning power to prevent drab realism from getting in the way of everything else and sprawling all over the action until it becomes incoherent and only shock tactics can beat it into shape.

I do not believe that any reading of the text, which lies on the page repetitively colloquial and colourless, could demonstrate the high quality of such a play. Perhaps that is why O'Neill was so often dismissed by poetic revivalists as too mediocre in diction to merit serious consideration. On the page, he is, and on the page, where much of their own work has since remained, the poetic revivalists were right. The new mid-century dramatists are in a stronger position. Although they have come up from below, with a bias in favour of the cruder stage effects, it has been acquired in the theatre. At least, like their American predecessors, they know where the issues are decided.

---

[2] ". . . the Sicilian, Giovanni Grasso, who exemplified a violent emotional acting that positively stunned us." *The Fervent Years*, by Harold Clurman (Dobson, 1946), p. 18.

robert brustein

WHY AMERICAN PLAYS
ARE NOT LITERATURE

One of the unique features of postwar American drama is its cheerful isolation from a central literary tradition. A successful playwright today may think of himself as a craftsman, an entertainer, even a creative artist, but only in very rare cases would he call himself a literary man. He does not share at all in those common interests — few enough in our society — which unite the novelist, poet, and essayist. In his subject matter, his writing style, his associations, his attitudes, and his ideas, the dramatist is far removed, if not completely cut off, from the mainstream of intellectual and literary discourse.

This lack of communication with the other disciplines gives the drama a peculiar insularity. The typical American playwright is encouraged to write, not by the pull of literary ideals, but by the stimulus of successful Broadway plays, and it is unusual when he develops beyond a hackneyed imitation of what is current and fashionable. Making his friends mainly within the theatrical profession, he rarely ventures out of it to have his mind refreshed. Unlike the novelist, he is almost never represented in the literary periodicals, and when he does communicate with the outside world it is generally through a short piece in the *New York Times* advertising his coming play with a reminiscence about how it came to be written.

Even our most important dramatists, past and present, have tended to remain firmly fixed within the confines of their own experience and craft. Besides plays, all the great European playwrights of the past hundred years wrote poetry, epics, novels, short stories, essays, or criticism; and in modern times dramatists like Brecht, Duerrenmatt, Beckett, Giraudoux, Synge, and O'Casey have moved freely among the other literary disciplines. With the exceptions of Thornton Wilder, Tennessee Williams (both former highbrows), and Arthur Miller, few American playwrights have made more than token gestures in the direction of non-dramatic literatures, while even fewer are aware of what is being attempted or said there. Specialization in America, insofar as it has affected the arts, has hit the drama hardest of all, cutting it off not only

Harper's Magazine, CCXIX (October, 1959), 167–172. Copyright by Robert Brustein.

from other literary traditions but from the very life which should be its subject matter.

This isolation can be partly attributed to the fact that American drama is a comparatively new expression, forced to create its tradition as it goes along. English playwrights like Wilde, Shaw, Eliot, and Osborne could draw on an already established dramatic heritage, one which includes the most distinguished names in literary history; in consequence, even minor dramatists like Barrie, Fry, Bridie, and Galsworthy, nourished by this strain, have created dramatic works which are eminently readable. The American drama, on the other hand — which seems to have sprung full-grown from the imagination of Eugene O'Neill — can still remember its own origins. In fact, O'Neill's persistent experimentation would seem to indicate that he was hurriedly trying to create a dramatic tradition for America which, like their gardens, took the English hundreds of years to produce. Borrowing from the drama of the Greeks, the Elizabethans, the Japanese, and nineteenth-century Europeans, O'Neill sought not native but cosmopolitan influences, and thus initiated a split from American literature which widens every year.

The split, of course, cuts both ways: American literary culture generally scorns the stage. In France, it is a rare thing when a novelist, poet, or philosopher does not express his themes in dramatic form, and it has long been the tradition for a French man of letters to include a volume or two of dramatic essays among his collected writings.

In America, on the other hand, theater criticism, abdicated by most intellectuals, has fallen into the hands of newspaper reviewers, while the drama itself is practically monopolized by commercial playwrights. Although the plays of writers like Camus, Sartre, Gide, Claudel, Mauriac, and Cocteau constitute an important part of their creative work, gifted American authors have, up till now, usually either ignored the drama totally or written badly in it. The quality of Fitzgerald's "The Vegetable," Hemingway's "The Fifth Column," and Wolfe's "Mannerhouse" — so far inferior to these authors' non-dramatic works — would seem to indicate that, unlike their French counterparts, American writers have not regarded the drama as a serious alternative form for the expression of their deepest convictions and insights.

If the American literary man has generally been indifferent, patronizing, or hostile toward the drama, some of the reasons for this indicate why our plays are so often outside the boundaries of literature. For there is a widespread conviction among men of mind that the dramatist, writing for an audience with debased values, does not have very high standards himself — and anxious to please a wide number, he creates a contaminated work which gives literature a bad name. Since the very structure of the drama is dependent on climactic emotional effects, it has often been accused of a fondness for bombast and sensationalism and of lacking intelligence and restraint — "an unmannerly daughter, showing a bad education," wrote Sir Philip Sidney hundreds of years ago, which "causeth her mother Poesy's honesty to be called in question." More frequently content to follow public taste than to lead it, the drama has developed an unsavory reputation through its alliance with the market place.

These traditional objections have become more vigorous in our own time as the drama has sought wider and less discriminating audiences. In the eighteenth century, when a play attracted a public for 62 performances, it was called the most prodigious success in history, while today a play must run for at least a year simply to make up costs. The non-creative unions — the press agents, managers, stagehands, and musicians — are squeezing the theater to death with excessive financial demands, and Broadway further exacerbates the situation with increasingly spectacular and expensive scenic effects guaranteed to excite spectator interest if all else fails. If union featherbedding were restrained, a play could again be successful after no more than 62 performances. And there is no telling how many honest works of imagination might see the stage without alteration. But the producer — rather than speculate on something risky and new — sticks to a tried-and-true formula based on the successes of the past. With the drama arbitrated by "show business," questions of finance overrule questions of taste, and it becomes harder to find financial support for anything which might "disturb" the audience.

The dramatist, as a result, discovers a number of non-literary partners looking over his shoulder as he writes, and this makes his work more than ever vulnerable to charges of artistic compromise. Compromise is not an essential of the collaborative enterprise — imagine the conductor of a symphony orchestra dictating elaborate changes in a musical composition for the sake of greater audience appeal. But it has now become second nature to Broadway, and few plays ever open there without having undergone strenuous revisions. While the novelist creates in the solitude of his own imagination, the dramatist re-creates with five or six worried production men at his elbow. Once paramount in importance, the playwright, in consequence, now finds his position overshadowed by the director whose power mushrooms every day; and even some of our most influential dramatists have been known to alter their work radically to retain the interest of a director who might insure its commercial success.

Since these alterations almost invariably result in a work of diminished honesty and complexity, writers whose artistic conscience demands greater satisfactions than commercial reward and the praise of newspaper reviewers view the theater with alarm and suspicion. Archibald

MacLeish is one of the few authors, not a professional playwright, who has regarded his occasional stage experience as a happy one, but then he seems to have adjusted nicely to the values of the medium in which he worked:

"I thought I was going to weep [when I heard] the Atkinson review [of 'J.B.']," he writes in a published letter to Kazan, and adds that the critical reception of the play was "general evidence that the problems *were* solved." When a work is primarily evaluated — as it is in our theater — by the enthusiastic applause of the majority, this is evidence indeed, and the distortions and convulsions to which a playwright's original ideas are submitted can be justified by a long line at the box office.

A very different response to theater experience comes from William Gibson, a literary man who looks on the success of his play, "Two for the Seesaw," as a hollow achievement reached by suppressing his true capabilities. Gibson, primarily a poet and novelist, has recorded his agonizing experience in *The Seesaw Log*, an illuminating account of the play's progress from idea to opening night. Like most serious writers, "it had been several years since [he] had taken a believing interest in the theater," but once having written a play his ultimate disenchantment was to come when he discovered as his collaborators not only the director, the producer, and the star, but the elevator man and probably the lavatory attendant as well. A writer to whom artistic integrity is a code of honor, he found that the perpetual revisions ordered in his play served only to cheapen it; and his original work eventually turned into a harmless diversion giving neither difficulty nor offense to anyone in the theater:

> Fifteen years earlier, when my work consisted of unpublished poems and a magazine asked me to change a word in one, I would not change a word; the poem went unpublished; it was a far cry to the present spate of rewriting to please. . . . I felt this of all of us, that in outgrowing our guardian angelship, and becoming reasonable citizens, we had lost some religious component in ourselves and this component was the difference between art and entertainment. . . . The theater, in this country, in this decade, [is] primarily a place not in which to be serious, but in which to be likable.

Mr. Gibson has accurately defined not only what distinguishes art from entertainment but literature from current drama. The silhouette of show business imposes itself on almost every work for our stage, and Broadway maintains its compulsive need to send the audience home in an affable frame of mind no matter what violence is done to the line of the play. With the writer constantly badgered to turn his play into the theatrical equivalent of a best seller, honest works of the imagination invariably become tainted with sentiment and dishonesty.

The director, of course, has a duty to request clarification of an author when his work is muddy, but more frequently revisions are a surrender to commodity demands. The famous changes in the last act of "Cat on a Hot Tin Roof," for example, had no bearing on the essential flaw of the play (which was the elusive ambiguity of the homosexual theme) but they did introduce into a bleak work a hopeful note of uplift compatible with Broadway's desire to remain well-liked. Since the trespassing of the director on the playwright's domain creates an atmosphere in which dramatic literature is very rarely produced, it remains the knottiest artistic dilemma of the American stage. It is not to be solved, as Tennessee Williams suggests, by having a "good psychiatrist in attendance at rehearsals," but rather by the playwright's strong resistance to commercial pressures when he is certain his work is being cheapened.

Of course, this resistance alone will not guarantee a play of high literary value. American drama is plagued by internal problems as well as external ones, and the dramatist will have to revise a number of his own attitudes if he wishes to create works of lasting power. One of these is his indifference to language. American drama, no matter how serious in intent, is very rarely readable, for our plays are often stage mechanisms which seem oddly wan and listless on the printed page. Only Tennessee Williams has consistently created a dramatic language which a good novelist might not be ashamed to have written, and even his style deteriorated in his last play. Most of our other playwrights, including our greatest, Eugene O'Neill, are charter members of a cult of inarticulacy, communicating high moments of thought and feeling not through speech but through dashes and exclamation points.

Playwrights are generally aware of this problem but do not consider it very important. Ever since the Elizabethan age, dramatists have been embarrassed when their plays appeared in print, but in the past they apologized for literary failings — today they caution the reader to ignore them and concentrate on dramatic values. Elmer Rice, who holds that "literary excellence is not an essential criterion in the evaluation of a play," goes even further in declaring that "words are not even necessary for the creation and communication of drama." Arthur Miller writes: "It is necessary to separate the drama from what we think of today as literature. A drama ought not to be looked at first and foremost from literary perspectives merely because it uses words, verbal rhythms, and poetic image." And Tennessee Williams defiantly defends "the incontinent blaze of a live theater, a theater meant for seeing and feeling." It is not surprising that Eugene O'Neill once blamed the failure of an early play on the fact that the actors had not emphasized the *silences* in the last act where the meaning of the play was to be found.

Nevertheless, to emphasize the drama's distinctness from literature is a defensible position if not carried too far. It is certainly true that plays are written primarily to be performed, and that writers who put inordinate emphasis on language to the exclusion of other important dramatic values have invariably produced works which are lifeless and dull on the stage. (I am thinking not only of closet dramatists like Robert Browning, Thomas Hardy, and Henry James but also of working playwrights like Sean O'Casey, whose later plays bog down in succulent and bloated rhetoric.) But both the finely jeweled style of closet drama and the shoddy language of our current plays are extremes. The dramatic form has always seemed to me the greatest literary form because it combines action *and* language. All of the great working dramatists of the past and present have been able to articulate their works, and there is still no better stage device than language for the unfolding of character and the revelation of dramatic insights. By permitting some scenes to be built out of actors' improvisations, certain playwrights abdicate their function entirely; and it is partly because of the playwright's indifference to language that our most conspicuous stage hero is brutal, inarticulate, and incapable of reflecting on his condition. The failure of dramatic language leads to a situation where a great many of our plays, including two of Mr. Miller's, conclude on a question — "Why?" — when it has traditionally been the dramatist's job to answer this question.

In other words, the murky language of our plays is a serious failing only insofar as it reflects our drama's basic failing, its murky thought. American plays are difficult to read because they so often yield little sense when they are read; in the quiet of the study one stumbles on inconsistencies, disharmonies, and contradictions which are sometimes ignored in the rapid excitement of performance. Those dramatists who are aware of this make an oblique admission of it by employing extra-dramatic techniques in the published plays in order to obscure the flaws. In some of the early plays of Eugene O'Neill, for example, extravagant stage directions are provided to sharpen points which have not been suitably dramatized, and Tennessee Williams also is sometimes given to lengthy parenthetical discussions of purpose, especially when he realizes he has ducked the very questions that his play has posed. As George Orwell has proved so emphatically, there is an intimate connection between language and ideas, and inadequate writing is often a sign either of confusion or evasion. In his compulsion to "move" the spectator no matter what happens to credibility or coherence, the American dramatist is further cut off from a literary tradition which is in our time experiencing an authentic renascence distinguished by its love and feeling for ideas.

As a consequence, American drama often seems to be the most mindless form of legitimate culture since eighteenth-century sentimental comedy, a form to which it bears more than a little resemblance.[1] I know of few professional American playwrights — Arthur Miller is a prominent exception — who would not consider it very odd to be called a thinker. On the contrary, most playwrights are devoted to dramatizing sensations which grow more hysterical and rarefied with every passing year.

In this, no doubt, they are trying to distinguish their work from what they consider the passionlessness of the English theater, and their vitality and energy have often had great value.

But this reaction can be carried too far. Tennessee Williams, for example — who calls himself a "feeling playwright" — is now indifferent to those dramatic works which, in embodying thought, are meant not only for performance but for reading and reflection, for he has developed an entirely different concept of a play:

> The color, the grace and levitation, the structural pattern in motion, and quick interplay of live beings, suspended like fitful lightning in a cloud, these things are the play, not words on paper, nor thoughts and ideas of an author, those shabby things snatched off basement counters at Gimbel's.

Beginning with a distaste for the logical, the abstruse, and the tendentious, Williams concludes by rejecting ideas altogether. He thus turns a truth into a half-truth, for there is a fruitful area between the ideological play and the play of pure sensation. In this area, two of Mr. Williams' major influences, Strindberg and D. H. Lawrence, produced some of their finest work. In fact, Mr. Williams' own place in the drama is secure not only because of his powerful "feeling" but because certain of his plays embodied provocative themes, while much of his later work is inferior because in relying too much on "fitful lightning" his thought is turgid and confused.

It should be clear that to introduce serious thought into the theater is not to rob it of passion; it is rather, by making that passion more meaningful, to impose greater burdens on the audience than a mere fingering of their emotions. I use the qualifying word "serious" because thought of one kind or another exists whether you like it or not — no work which uses words and action can be totally free from ideas. Even the most unintellectual forms — such as the farces of Labiche — have an idea at their base, if only a maxim by Rochefoucauld. Broadway is depressing not

[1] I quote from Oliver Goldsmith who, in attacking the sentimental dramatists in 1772, might have been describing American domestic plays like "The Dark at the Top of the Stairs" or "Raisin in the Sun": "These comedies have had of late a great success, perhaps from their novelty, and also from their flattering every man in his favorite foible. In these plays almost all the characters are good, and exceedingly generous. . . . If they happen to have faults or foibles, the spectator is taught, not only to pardon, but to applaud them, in consideration of the goodness of their hearts."

because ideas are not enunciated there but because these ideas invariably *are* "snatched off basement counters at Gimbel's." Pretentious, eva-
sive, and rarely free from formula, the falsification of Broadway thought
inevitably results in the falsification of its passion. Our farces are no
longer amoral and destructively funny but now embody homilies and
sentiment while our melodramas revolve around drug addiction or the
pernicious psychic influence of Mom. Our serious drama is informed by
a debased Freudianism, our comedies are set in motion by man-chasing
women, and our musicals — with one or two exceptions like "West Side
Story" and "My Fair Lady" — are produced by people who write about
Love while thinking about Money. There are hardly two plays each
year which are not obsessively biological in their themes, yet for all this
preoccupation none have any real sexual interest. Homosexuality, promiscuity, infidelity, incest — all these considerations are toyed with but
always sentimentalized or evaded. The result is that we have a theater
which will not admit the simple truths that everyone discusses in the
living-room.

Almost all of our drama, in fact, is equivocal or needlessly ambiguous, for our dramatists find it difficult to square the passionate aspects of
their plays with their ideas about American life. One frequently finds,
consequently, contradictions between the psychological and the social or
the emotional and mental aspects of a play. O'Neill squeezes an attack
on American capitalism into a romantic play about Marco Polo; Arthur
Miller tries to document the effect of McCarthyism on the American
public through an obfuscating treatment of the Salem witch trials;
Tennessee Williams drags a Southern segregationist into the middle of a
sexual nightmare; and Archibald MacLeish superimposes his feelings
about the hydrogen bomb on a religious drama adapted from the Book
of Job.

Though each of these dramatists is concerned with some specific
fact of American life, none is able to speak concretely about it for fear
that his work will somehow lose its "universality"; but as any good literary man can tell them nothing is more "universal" than a careful presentation of the particular. (Saul Bellow's Chicago Jew, Augie March,
is more American in his special and concrete experience than any of the
universalized figures of our postwar drama.) A direct confrontation of
American life — banished from our stage — has had to find refuge in
"illegitimate" theatrical entertainments like the monologues of Mort Sahl,
the night-club skits of May and Nichols, and an occasional review at the
Downstairs Room.

There is, in other words, very little that is contemporary about our
contemporary drama. Most of our plays, for all the light they throw on

American life, might have been written by a Visigoth in the Year 1, while the others merely parrot the liberal prejudices of the audience or hide their meaning (if it is disturbing or controversial) under a mountain of allegory. In this self-imposed censorship, our dramatists demonstrate the most severe consequences of their alienation from intellectual discourse; for in our theater, as it is now constituted, there is little to stimulate the more ambitious playwright. Postwar American drama is stationary, and its fondness for formal experimentation (generally designed to obscure sentiment, banality, or sheer confusion) merely gives it an illusion of movement. America today has no theatrical *avant-garde*, only two dramatists worthy of note, and no one among the younger writers to ruffle a few feathers with radical and exciting new ideas. The intellectual ferment provided in the past by O'Neill, Odets, and Lillian Hellman is practically nonexistent today, and our drama is daily growing more narrow and circumscribed, strangling itself in its own living-room.

Arthur Miller is the one American playwright with the ambition to write a mature drama which transcends the family crisis, the sexual conflict, and the individual psychosis; yet in his uttterances about "the people" and "the common man" he sometimes sounds as if his social thinking has not yet progressed past the 'thirties. Since he is an artist with substantial gifts and a real affection for ideas, it seems a waste that some of his own plays should suffer from the very defects he observes in the plays of others; and it is very possible that these defects might have been avoided or overcome if there had been more opportunity for debate, conversation, and intercourse with his equals in the other disciplines.

I harp on these inter-disciplinary influences not just to make an academic point but because there is evidence that American drama may soon be refreshed from non-dramatic sources. The younger novelists of the 'fifties, whose work has such distinction and intelligence, are beginning to show some inclination to knock down the prevailing borders between literature and the drama. Norman Mailer and James Baldwin are both writing plays which are certain, in different ways, to be exciting and unusual; and Lillian Hellman and Lester Osterman are currently encouraging writers like Saul Bellow, Herbert Gold, and James Purdy to write plays as well.

If these writers can transfer to the stage some of the incisive knowledge of American life they display in their novels, if they can submit themselves to the fearfully difficult discipline of the dramatic form, and if producers can be found who will support their works without trying to commercialize them, we may soon have a substantial group of exciting and controversial playwrights. Even more, we may soon have a drama which will set new standards of honesty, intelligence, and excellence for our practicing playwrights, and which will turn the theater once again into a place — not just to be likable — but serious and profound.

edd winfield parks

EUGENE O'NEILL'S QUEST

For some twenty years (1936–1956), Eugene O'Neill's expressionistic dramas with their symbolic distortion of objective facts to reveal inner experiences were more popular in South America and especially in the Scandinavian countries than they were at home. The dramatist who in the 1920s had been awarded three Pulitzer Prizes was regarded mainly as of historical importance when in 1936 he was the recipient of the Nobel Prize. To many critics, it seemed a recognition (belated or, perhaps, undeserved) of work that might once have been exciting but that no longer seemed vital or particularly relevant. In the main, we failed to see in his work what the Scandinavians found in it.

Since 1956, there has been a tremendous upsurge of interest in O'Neill's plays. When *The Iceman Cometh* was produced in New York in 1946, it met with an exceedingly cool reception; ten years later, it was a brilliant success. So, at least as far as surface recognition was concerned, were the autobiographical plays, *A Moon for the Misbegotten* and *Long Day's Journey into Night,* as well as the historical play, *A Touch of the Poet.* The rather grim story of a tubercular prostitute, *Anna Christie,* has been turned into a musical comedy; the tragic *Desire Under the Elms* has been turned into a movie that follows with reasonable faithfulness the play itself and the movie script that O'Neill once prepared from it (the substitution of a foreign for a New England girl was made by O'Neill in the script).

This may be no more than jumping on the bandwagon, although only the musical comedy really seems a misguided and hardboiled attempt to gain financial advantage from a newly-found popularity. Yet

Tulane Drama Review, IV (1960), 99–107. Copyright 1960 by *Tulane Drama Review;* reprinted by permission of the *Tulane Drama Review* and the author.

there is little to indicate that we have yet recognized the ideas behind O'Neill's plays — the ideas that today make him a living force in Sweden, Denmark, and Brazil. We have concentrated too much on the sense of doom and futility that pervades O'Neill's work. Undeniably this negative aspect is there. The man who was always "a little in love with death" was assuredly not an optimist when he dealt with life. Yet a reading of O'Neill plays indicates that he is not basically a deterministic writer, but rather that he has been attempting to find a philosophy that would reconcile a rationalistic view of the universe with man's need for something beyond rationalism — for a sense of the infinite beyond the finite.

Early in his career, O'Neill recognized this basic necessity, when he wrote in an essay that "the playwright today must dig at the roots of the sickness of today as he feels it — the death of the old God and the failure of science and materialism to give any satisfying new one for the surviving primitive religious instinct to find a meaning for life in." In the attempt to find that meaning and to state it in dramatic terms, O'Neill has temporarily embraced and then discarded many modern substitutes for religion, and has even attempted to re-state the Catholic concept of religion in the terms of modern psychology. Essentially he has been a mystic who used the trappings of realism, but a mystic uneasily aware that with the advent of scientific determinism came the need for a new symbolism.

For a new day in man's thought, a new and fresh power was needed. An instinctive, convinced belief in mythological gods and heroes (Hebraic as well as Scandinavian or Greek) was past; even the moral order no longer carried a vital power. Instead, that power was to be found in the scientific laws which were the true if inanimate rulers of the universe. Writers could no longer accept the myths of yesterday, as Herman Melville earlier had recognized when he wrote that "great geniuses are a part of their times; they themselves are the times, and possess a corresponding coloring." So for *Moby Dick* Melville used a scientific and natural symbolism: he took for a springboard into his exploration of the unknowable soul not an outworn mythology but the sea and a man's search for an actual and a symbolic white whale. Nature became the tragic force, and Moby Dick the *deus ex machina*. O'Neill's great master, Henrik Ibsen, made heredity a tragic force in *Ghosts;* however unjust it might be, it led as surely to irrevocable doom as ever the moral order had. These and many other writers created powerful literary conventions out of the scientific thought of the time.

O'Neill also has followed these modern conventions. In his first important play, *The Moon of the Caribbees,* he set man against nature, with the spirit of the sea intended to be the hero, and the man Smitty reduced to silhouetted gestures of self-pity. Smitty's sentimental posings, set against the revealing moods of the sea's eternal truth, reveal that he is out of harmony with nature and therefore no longer attuned to beauty. Only the noble savage, or in our time the natural man, can attain this harmony. O'Neill stated this theme explicitly when he tried to explain the meaning of a difficult and to many people a confusing play: the protagonist of *The Hairy Ape* is "a symbol of man, who has lost his old harmony with nature, the harmony which he used to have as an animal and has not acquired in a spiritual way . . . The public saw just the stoker, not the symbol, and the symbol makes the play either important or just another play . . . The subject here is the same ancient one that always was and always will be the one subject for drama, and that is man and his struggle with his own fate. The struggle used to be with the gods, but is now with himself, his own past, his attempt 'to belong'."

O'Neill temporarily abandoned this immediate symbol, but throughout the plays the ultimate longing and the ultimate symbol remain the same: man's desire to find a satisfactory spiritual peace, a place "to belong" not only in this world but in relation to the universe. The quest was in part at least a personal one. Much later he was to write of himself that "I will always be a stranger who never feels at home . . . who can never belong."

For dramatic purposes, however, he turned back to the theme of man's struggle against nature; out of it, in fact, he wrote one of his greatest plays, *Ile*. Here a tight, just, hard-fisted New England sea captain who has failed for the first time to secure his quota of whale oil is faced with mutiny, and with the prospect of a wife slowly going insane from loneliness and fear; but when the ice breaks and the whales spout, the captain turns inevitably to the chase. The background is deliberately meager. All the overtones, the true background, are in the struggle shadowed forth rather than expressed between man and his ancient enemy, nature. As in all great plays there are two conflicts: the internal struggle in Captain Keeney between pride and compassion; the external struggle between a captain and his crew, a husband and his wife, a man and the universe. Because he is above all else the primitive man, the proud hunter, Captain Keeney makes his decision; and relentlessly, with nature as inexorable as ever were the Greek gods, tragedy results.

The play was satisfying, but to O'Neill the philosophy behind it was not. Man's spirit had to be reckoned with, as well as man's mind. Always the spirit seeks an assurance of immortality. If a rationalistic and mechanistic philosophy denies and to the rational mind proves that it cannot be found through religion, that the assurance can no longer be achieved through faith, then it must be sought elsewhere. In his own search, O'Neill fell temporarily under the sway of the idea that a man attains immortality through his descendants. This is the underlying motif of *The Fountain*. In a program note, O'Neill told the audience that "The idea of writing a 'Fountain' came on finally from my interest in the recurrence in folklore of the beautiful legend of a healing spring of eternal youth." So Ponce de Leon searches fruitlessly for this spring which will wash away the years and give him an earthly immortality; at last, when he has given up hope, he finds a vicarious immortality in the youth of his nephew: "One must accept, absorb, give back, become oneself a symbol."

This is the clearest affirmation that O'Neill's philosophy at that time could admit. The fountain was a symbol of life, tossing its little drops, its human beings, high in the air. They had myriad shapes and colors: some were caught in the light, others dropped dully back, and a few burst into an incandescent miniature rainbow. It did not greatly matter: more drops must be propagated that more drops may be tossed into the air, and absorbed back again into the whole.

Yet there is something more. According to this belief, the creative power, the strongest power in nature, would perform the age-long functions of mythic religion. For the man this concept was not finally satisfying; for the dramatist it proved exceedingly fruitful. It is out of this theme of creation and continuance that he wrote two of his finest plays, *The Great God Brown* and *Mourning Becomes Electra*. Even when he parallels, and deliberately suggests cross-comparison with, the ancient Greek legend of Electra, O'Neill endows his characters with psychological complications that we recognize (and he intends us to recognize) by such modern terms as repressions, frustrations, and fixations. But men and women today, like those in ancient Greece, can not resist forces stronger than themselves: the terms have changed, but the tragedy remains the same. In this play with its American setting and modern time of action, O'Neill is attempting to rephrase the motivations of classical tragedy so as to relate them to our own doubts, fears, and desires, but in the process to give us, also, faith in the creative life force.

In *The Great God Brown*, this is combined with the more dominant motif of the religion of art. O'Neill defines his purpose in this play as showing "the mystery any one man or woman can feel but not understand as the meaning of any event — or accident — in any life on earth." To give added depth, richness, and suggestiveness, he deliberately mixed what we think of as folklore and as revealed religion: Dion Anthony is in part Dionysius, and in part St. Anthony, and he returns for strength to Cybele, the pagan earth mother. But this mystical element serves to accentuate the importance of the individual, even as the use of masks to indicate an actor's public or private character emphasizes an individual's complexity. But one person is influenced and changed by others even as he acts upon them, as we grope in the world's half-light for a fuller illumination. Here the reader can identify himself with the characters, can fully comprehend the nature and intensity of their desires, whether or not he accepts the underlying philosophy.

That is not possible with all his plays, at least for most of us. O'Neill has embraced even more dubious philosophies. In *Dynamo* he envisioned a man who saw a new god in the whirling wheels of machinery and the weird power of electricity, but this study of a fantastic modernly-grounded religious mania was neither dramatically nor philosophically convincing. O'Neill also flirted briefly and tentatively with Marxianism in *Marco Millions,* but it was at best a half-hearted flirtation since he was, soon afterward, describing Communism as "the most grotesque god that ever came out of Asia." Sociological nostrums, especially the theory that man will quickly improve if only his environment be changed for the better, won his half-hearted allegiance in such plays as *All God's Chillun Got Wings* and *Desire Under the Elms.*

Whether his philosophical ideas had proved satisfying or not, he had consistently attempted to get beyond the literal and factual reality. Both the man and the dramatist seem ever in quest of a valid, tenable explanation of the meaning of life. In that quest he came to Christian Catholicism, and out of it he wrote the moving but only partially successful *Days Without End.* In this play meaning inheres not in the fountain or the dynamo or the sexual delta, but in the crucifix. He has not abandoned modern terms or modern psychology, and he continues to be concerned with man's essential dualism to such an extent that the two parts of the main character are played by two different actors. Somehow, too, there is little difference in the terms of his Christian characters and those of his earlier non-Christian ones: John Loving believes with the rationalistic part of his mind that "we are all the slaves of meaningless chance," but with the idealistic part that "a new Savior must be born who will reveal to us how we can be saved from ourselves."

If the play has too much of dramatic and philosophical debate in it to be quite successful as a drama, it is the clearest statement we have of O'Neill's constant striving to find a satisfactory philosophy of life. It gives in epitome his own spiritual evolution: he is seeking the infinite behind the finite, searching for something that will add to the dignity of man. Whatever the terms employed, however unsatisfactory the explanations, O'Neill holds in this play that man's spirit is greater and ultimately more important than man's body. If at times he seems only to have a faith that man must have a faith, he has made an honest and unrelenting search for valid and tenable bases for a faith that will not deny scientific truths but will affirm a deeper, more positive spiritual truth.

"Man is involved in a web of circumstance, a web that is not of his

own weaving." O'Neill had begun as a playwright with this deterministic philosophy of life and the universe; rather disconcertingly, he
has partially reverted to it in his later plays. The disturbed and disturbing state of the world shook his lightly-rooted faith; even more directly, a serious personal illness in 1934 temporarily ended his dramatic
activity; it developed into, or was later diagnosed as, the incurable,
slowly ravaging Parkinson's Disease.

It may be too early to evaluate the work of O'Neill's darker years,
but certain unmistakable trends seem dominant. He had turned back into
his own past for dramatic material; increasingly he pinned his faith on
human love and warmth to give a meaning to life; and he presented
man lacking the will to act as being spiritually dead, however alive
physically he might be. There is a cathartic quality in these plays, but
the purging clearly was intended more for the author than for the audience: O'Neill was attempting to objectify by writing out of himself certain obsessive memories that long had haunted him.

This is made manifest in the brief, moving foreword to *Long Day's
Journey*, cast in the form of a letter to his wife Carlotta: "Dearest: I give
you the original script of this play of old sorrow, written in tears and
blood. A sadly inappropriate gift, it would seem, for a day celebrating
happiness. But you will understand. I mean it as a tribute to your love
and tenderness which gave me the faith in love that enabled me to face
my dead at last and write this play — write it with deep pity and understanding and forgiveness for all the four haunted Tyrones."

Eugene includes himself among the haunted, and he makes no attempt except for changing names to disguise the autobiographical nature
of the play. James Tyrone is an immensely popular actor, embittered
because he has sacrificed the chance of greatness for immediate popularity, and seeking wealth through ill-timed real estate speculations; Mary
Tyrone is a drug addict because her husband employed an incompetent,
inexpensive doctor at the younger son's birth, and the doctor gave her
opium to quiet her pains; James Junior is a dipsomaniac, a wastrel, and
a jealous-hearted failure. The tightly-knit action takes place on the day
when Edmund (or Eugene) is admitted to have tuberculosis, and is to
be sent to a sanitarium.

Of these four, only Eugene has a chance to achieve salvation of any
kind in this world. His sickness is physical; his moral nature, although
warped, is fundamentally sound. But the sickness in father, mother, and
brother is essentially a moral sickness: in seeking to escape from the
world they have grown egocentric, cold; their flashes of warmth are
sporadic and to a degree irrational; they have lost the capacity to love
and the will to act. Man seeks always for serenity and order, for a sense
of belonging, in a mysteriously alien universe. Mary fancies she might

have found it if she had become a nun; James, if he had not prostituted his acting ability; James Junior, if he had achieved something — he is not sure quite what. These hopeless escapist fancies lead them inevitably into the past, away from the present; and ahead of them is only the darkly symbolic night.

It is a powerfully written, integrated tragedy, but the motivating force behind each of these tragic figures derives not from nobility or even ignoble ambition but from insufficiency. In earlier, more objective plays O'Neill used many devices to point up the contrast between appearance and reality; he levied upon psychology to present an awareness of the difference between conscious and subconscious realities. Here the devices are relatively straightforward, but the psychological twistings and turnings are exceedingly complex as the characters attempt to conceal their real thoughts and motivations not only from each other but from themselves, until driven by some compulsive inner force to confess the subconscious reality.

There is something of the detective story technique in thus using action to conceal rather than to reveal character. This similarity of method appears even more clearly in *A Moon*, where a virgin deliberately masquerades as a loose woman and her warm-hearted old Irish father hides a basic goodness under apparent meanness and gruffness. This too is an intensely personal work, for the protagonist is James Tyrone, Junior, and incidents briefly described in *Long Day's Journey* are in *A Moon* developed and made a necessary part of the dramatic action. It is set later in time. Mrs. Tyrone had died in California; on the train bringing her body east, her son seeks forgetfulness and peace in an alcoholic orgy with a prostitute. This should not be read as strictly biographical: O'Neill needed one specfic dramatic incident to focus and pin-point James's remorse at having betrayed himself as well as his mother, but this is only the ultimate betrayal. The young man who could not enjoy horse-racing because of impatience to get back to his hotel room and his solitary drinking had already succumbed: the incident is needed dramatically to underline and make concrete his loss of values, but it only emphasizes the subconscious reality by making apparent the conscious reality.

O'Neill's theme of death in life re-appears, even more explicitly. Phil and Josie Hogan are alive because they have warmth and the ability to love; James is empty, and Josie cradling the man who has fallen asleep in her arms perceptively remarks, "God forgive me, it's a fine end to all my scheming, to sit here with the dead hugged to my breast, and the silly mug of the moon grinning down, enjoying the joke." As human beings Josie and her father have many defects, but they have also a quality of aliveness that James has killed in himself, so that Josie tenderly and pityingly can wish only for the man she loves, "May you have your wish and die in your sleep soon, Jim, darling. May you rest forever in forgiveness and peace."

The title implies that James had never at any time had any real chance to be different, to control his own destiny. He was misbegotten truly, whereas Josie is so only because she has freely given her love to an emotionally-dead man incapable of returning that love. Is this a sibling's pity for an older brother, or an attitude toward life? The intensely personal nature of the play, the felt need of catharsis for the author, makes interpretation doubly difficult. Yet clearly O'Neill believes that it is not enough to be loved; one must be capable of giving out as well as of taking in if one is to be saved, in this world or the next. In these two plays there is no hint that salvation may be won by a faith or a philosophy, for all the values are personal ones. The person rather than the idea, O'Neill seems to be saying, gives a meaning to life.

Since it is less subjective, *The Iceman Cometh* should provide a better test as to meaning than the autobiographical works. Unfortunately the tone is that of the dream-phantasia, and expressionistic distortion has been carried so far that the philosophical line of thought has been obscured. From the heavily ironic title, with the iceman or death substituted for the life-giving bridegroom, to the commentary that these are men "scared of life, but even more scared of dying," the tone and the action emphasize this note of hopeless waiting.

The group of men in Harry Hope's saloon, back in 1912, have diverse backgrounds but all have two items in common: each has in his past a cankerous secret that has so corrupted him that he has lost the will to act and the power to make decisions; each has taken refuge in a deadening alcoholic daze (only Hemingway's literary characters equal O'Neill's as two-handed drinkers, but even Hemingway does not make drinking the avenue to mental escape that O'Neill does). As the play opens, they are waiting for a hardware salesman, Hickey, who in the past has without really disturbing them managed to give them a transitory joyousness, an illusion of aliveness. This time when Hickey appears he introduces a disturbingly new note, for he has acquired the will to act, and he has acted. He is an irritating stimulus, goading each man to act, goading each man compulsively to reveal the secret that haunts him. Each makes an abortive effort to face reality. When Hickey's freedom-giving action is revealed as the murder of the wife whom he had subconsciously hated for her goodness, the men passively subside into their accustomed and reasonably painless alcoholic waiting.

This is a curious reversal of the other two plays. Here it is the person who deprives life of its meaning, as though O'Neill were presenting the other side of the same coin. In *Long Day's Journey* Edmund at least has warmth and potentialities; in *A Moon* Josie and Phil Hogan have warmth and an inner if well-concealed integrity. The denials and nega- tions are set against affirmations. In *The Iceman* there is at best only a negative affirmation: that these men are essentially dead because in their egocentricity they have lost the qualities that give a meaning to life. They are no longer capable of human love, or even the will to act. Each one re- veals the conscious act and the subconscious reasons behind the act that have deprived him of the power to make and carry out a decision. Insofar as each was responsible for his own action, the play is not deterministic. But O'Neill never really indicates how much choice a man had, or how far he was simply a puppet in the web of circumstances — and of circum- stances not of his own making.

A Touch of the Poet is related to these highly personal dramas only in that O'Neill continues to use the dream-motif as a means of denying or evading the too-harsh realities of life. The time is 1828; the setting a village tavern near Boston. Cornelius Melody, ex-Major, ex-gentleman, and presently tavern-keeper, lives in his memories of earlier gallantry in love and war; as his realistic daughter ironically remarks: "God help you, it must be a wonderful thing to live in a fairy tale where only dreams are real to you." When the dream is shattered, when Melody is inexorably forced to admit to himself his actual situation, the man dies even while he continues to live. His wife recognizes this all too clearly when she tells her daughter: "Look at the dead face on him, Sara. He's like a corpse."

Even in this non-autobiographical play, O'Neill's quest for a valid faith has shifted from the philosophical to the personal. The wife and daughter are vital because they have the human warmth to give them- selves completely to love. In the autobiographical plays this contrast between emotional life and emotional death is made even more explicit. In one sense, O'Neill as dramatist had changed radically. He was less interested in digging at the roots of the world's sickness than in delving directly into his own mental and spiritual past. That the values he ex- pressed dramatically are also values that had personal meaning is par- tially borne out by the concluding paragraph to his wife, in *Long Day's Journey*: "These twelve years, Beloved One, have been a Journey into Light — into love."

With human love there is light. Implicit in these plays, also, are overtones suggesting that human love is in itself divine, that as long as man retains inside himself warmth and feeling his plight is known to an understanding and forgiving God. Especially near the end of *Long Day's Journey* are these transcendental overtones heard, in Eugene's handling of the baffling, tragic inter-relationships in his own family. In this re- spect he seems nearer to a Catholic fatalism than to scientific deter- minism. He has described (through Edmund) in his own life occasional mystical experiences when "the moment of ecstatic freedom came. The peace, the end of the quest, the last harbor, the joy of belonging to a fulfillment beyond men's lousy, pitiful, greedy fears and hopes and dreams . . . Like a saint's vision of beatitude. Like the veil of things as they seem drawn back by an unseen hand. For a second you see — and seeing the secret, are the secret. For a second there is meaning! Then the hand lets the veil fall and you are alone, lost in the fog again, and you stumble on toward nowhere, for no good reason!!"

This is the dilemma, the grim dichotomy that O'Neill has struggled with and never quite mastered. With his rational mind he has seen men struggling on toward nowhere, but he has seen also (possibly not with his eyes) that they both see the secret and are the secret. In rationalistic determinism nothing is hidden, eventually, to the finite mind, for the reason that there is nothing unseen. If O'Neill's visions were momentary, sporadic, and unconnected, he felt nevertheless that those visions were real — as actual as, say, the eating of bread or drinking of wine. As his faith in the abstract idea or the philosophic or theological doctrine waned, he substituted for it the warmth of human love. However un-orthodox an approach to divinity this may be, it gives a mellow under-lying richness to the otherwise-dark autobiographical plays.

tom f. driver

STRENGTH AND WEAKNESS IN ARTHUR MILLER

Arthur Miller's introduction to his *Collected Plays* (New York, 1957) is one of the major documents of American theatre. It reveals an eminent playwright having struggled to understand and perfect his craft. It shows him eager to use the theatre to express his evolving ideas. It shows his strengths, and also his weaknesses.

The foremost asset Arthur Miller possesses as a playwright is his knowledge that the theatre must dedicate itself to public matters. He has

Tulane Drama Review, IV (1960), 45–52. Copyright 1960 by *Tulane Drama Review*; reprinted by permission of the *Tulane Drama Review* and the author.

an acute sense of his audience as persons to be addressed, never merely spectators to be tolerated. "A play," he writes, "ought to make sense to common-sense people . . . the only challenge worth the effort is the widest one and the tallest one, which is the people themselves."

His writing, although it usually has an axe to grind, does not attempt to startle society with new ideas. Indeed, he does not believe that the theatre *can* promulgate entirely new ideas, because it must gather the assent of its audience as it moves along, and this is impossible with the radically new. The theatre should enunciate "not-yet-popular ideas which are already in the air, ideas for which there has already been a preparation by non-dramatic media." Thus he understands the vigor of theatrical art to depend in part on its timeliness: drama is "the art of the present tense par excellence." It follows that the theatre binds isolated human beings into their essential corporateness: "I regard the theatre as a serious business, one that makes or should make man more human, which is to say, less alone."

A corollary of this "public" view of theatre is the belief that psychology is an insufficient basis for it. Psychology becomes preoccupied with the individual, in many cases even the idiosyncratic, whereas the proper concerns of the theatre are social. Miller says that he himself has "shown a preference for plays which seek causation not only in psychology but in society."

If one takes the "public" view of theatre seriously, he will be forced to ponder the nature of dramatic action and, with it, the importance of the handling of time in the structuring of a play. It has often been said that the problem of dramatic construction is the problem of handling exposition, a truism Miller repeats when he writes, in discussing Ibsen, that "the biggest single dramatic problem" is "how to dramatize what has gone before." It is something other than a truism, however, when he adds:

> I say this not merely out of technical interest, but because dramatic characters, and the drama itself, can never hope to attain a maximum degree of consciousness unless they contain a viable unveiling of the contrast between past and present, and an awareness of the process by which the present has become what it is.

Miller rightly perceives that one of Ibsen's greatest strengths lay in his ability to manage theatrical time so as to express the sequence of causation which he saw in the lives of the characters in his plays. Miller also sees that re-arrangement of time-sequences is tantamount to a change in the implied causal relationships between events. It was just because the notion of causation was so different in *All My Sons* from what it came to be in *Death of a Salesman* that the former remained an "old fashioned" play of exposition, confrontation, and climax, whereas the latter involved "an explosion of watch and calendar," with a corresponding change in the level of reality to which it appealed.

It is hardly possible to read Miller without being impressed with his desire to see and report life realistically. He tells us that when he was writing *A Memory of Two Mondays,* he desired "to be abrupt, clear, and explicit in setting forth fact as fact and art as art so that the sea of theatrical sentiment, which is so easily let in to drown all shape, meaning, and perspective, might be held back and some hard outline of a human dilemma be allowed to rise and stand." Even though there is melodrama in *All My Sons, The Crucible,* and *A View from the Bridge,* it is difficult to reflect on Miller's work without feeling that a hard realism is informing most, if not all, of his concrete observations.

It is the more to his credit as a thinker that his notion of the real is not limited by the canons of what has come to be known in the theatre as "realism." He is quite aware that multiple meanings are attached to the word "real," and while his bent of mind seems to prevent him from investigating the concept of "the real" philosophically, he is far from assuming that the only reality is the positive concrete:

> The longer I dwelt on the whole spectacle, [human dedication to evil] the more clear became the failure of the present age to find a universal moral sanction, and the power of realism's hold on our theatre was an aspect of this vacuum. For it began to appear that our inability to break more than the surfaces of realism reflected our inability — playwrights and audiences — to agree upon the pantheon of forces and values which must lie behind the realistic surfaces of life. In this light, realism, as a style, could seem to be a defense against the assertion of meaning. How strange a conclusion this is when one realizes that the same style seventy years ago was the prime instrument of those who sought to illuminate meaning in the theatre. . . .

Miller describes the way his research into the Salem witch trials led him to understand the limited frame of reference in which modern realistic discourse must be carried on. Out of this came his subsequent attempt to go beyond the limitations of realistic theatre. Is is an enlightening tale of a pragmatic mind's discovery of the usefulness of religious language.

What Miller asks for is a theatre of "heightened consciousness." He speaks of two passions in man, the "passion to feel" and the "passion to know." It is his conviction that we need, and can have, more of the latter. "Drama is akin to the other inventions of man in that it ought to help us to know more, and not merely to spend our feelings." The experience of writing *The Crucible* seems to have shown him that a theatre given more to objective knowledge, to heightened self-awareness, is possible. He mentions Brecht as one who has tackled the central problem of contemporary drama, "which is again the problem of consciousness." And in speaking of *Death of a Salesman,* he has the courage to mention its chief limitation when he asks, "but was there not another realm even higher, where feeling took awareness more openly by the hand and both equally ruled and were illuminated?"

These, then, are the strengths of Arthur Miller: an acute awareness of the "public" nature of theatre, the desire to see and report life realistically, an unwillingness to settle for a merely positivist version of reality, and a desire to see a theatre of "heightened consciousness." By putting these concerns before the public, Arthur Miller has shown that his sights are higher than those of any of his competitors at the Broadway box-office. The fact that such concerns exist in a playwright of his prominence is proof that our theatre is still alive.

It is perhaps unfair to judge Miller's work as a playwright by his own critical standard. To do so, however, will reveal not only the deficiencies of much American theatre but will also be a way of seeing certain weaknesses that lie in Miller's thought.

We must remember that the only success both popular and critical Miller has had in this country is *Death of a Salesman.* We must also remember that it remains more consistently upon the level of psychology and feeling than do any of his other plays. The original title for it was *The Inside of His Head,* and the objective, apparently, was to create a dramatic form which "would literally be the process of Willy Loman's way of mind." The result was the kind of play, says Miller, which "issues in a genuine poetry of feeling," and in which feeling is "raised up as the highest good and the ultimate attainment in drama."

It was beyond this level that he wished to go in achieving that other realm, "where feeling took awareness more openly by the hand." Yet when he attempted that other realm in *The Crucible* and *A View from the Bridge,* he was not successful. After *A View from the Bridge* failed in New York, it was revised and later played successfully in London; but it is instructive to note that the revisions were all in the direction of making the psychology of the central character more prominent. Indeed, it had been obvious all along that, although the author of *A View from the Bridge* had wanted to write a play in which action took precedence over psychology, he had chosen for this purpose a character and situation bound to interest the audience primarily from a psychological point of view. It was the story of a Brooklyn longshoreman unconsciously in love with his niece, a man who destroys all his family because of jealousy.

In classical times, such a theme might have served a trans-psychological purpose; but in Miller's play there was no level of meaning, law, providence, or fate, upon which an action that transcended character might rest. The action inevitably fell back, as it were, into the subjectivity of Eddie and his uncontrollable jealousy. No genuine parallel with the Greek drama had been found. In the case of Oedipus, for instance, the objective realm is clearly expressed in the problem of the health of the Theban *polis*, the proscriptions against patricide and incest, and the search for truth as a self-evident good. Nothing on this level was present in *A View from the Bridge*, yet without it no theatre of action rather than character is possible. Mr. Miller had not, in short, solved the problem of "the failure of the present age to find a universal moral sanction," and without such a solution, in one degree or another, there was nothing other than psychology to support the action of his play.

From this experience Mr. Walter Kerr would doubtless argue, as he does in *How Not to Write a Play*, that it is only psychological consistency and the creation of interesting character which makes good plays, and that the one undoubted success of Arthur Miller, *Death of a Salesman*, shows it. All that it really shows, however, is that Arthur Miller is typical of our theatre in being able to do character best and in not being able to sustain a more comprehensive kind of action.

Two weaknesses are fatal to Miller's attempt to write the kind of objective theatre he sees is needed. First, his view of man in society is too narrow. He is restricted, as many have pointed out, by a particular social theory which he seems not to have had the inclination to probe until it yielded him a fundamental idea of human nature. Brecht, to take an opposite example, did such probing. Apparently Miller's Marxism changes as he goes along, and it would be going beyond the evidence to suggest that he adheres to any "line," whether political or ideological. Nevertheless, he bears a quasi-Marxist stamp and most of his plays tend to become mere partisan social critique. The momentary usefulness of that social critique, or the extent to which it actually is Marxist, is nothing to the point. The point is simply that his conception of the "reality" with which man must deal is limited.

Miller has some lofty things to say about *All My Sons* being an attack upon "unrelatedness" and about crime "having roots in a certain relationship of the individual to society;" but when all is said and done, the play seems to be only a play about an aircraft-parts manufacturer in wartime. It has rapidly become dated. The mistake was not in being timely, but in being timely with too simple a point of view. *The Crucible* invited the immediate application to the McCarthy issue which it received, and which made it seem small. When it was revived in 1958 off Broadway, it did have more success than in its first run during the McCarthy era. Even then, however, I found the play strident, written with an emotion inappropriate to its inner life.

> Our drama is condemned, so to speak, to the emotions of subjectivism, which, as they approach knowledge and self-awareness, become less and less actual and real to us. In retrospect, I think that my course in *The Crucible* should have been toward greater self-awareness and not, as my critics have implied, toward an enlarged and more pervasive subjectivism.

The goal is right. It is not reached because Miller's sense of objectivity is not comprehensive enough. He lacks that metaphysical inquisitiveness which would take him to the bottom of the problems he encounters. One might say that he sees the issues too soon, sees them in their preliminary form of social or even moral debate, but not in terms of dramatic events that disturb the audience's idea of basic truth, which is the foundation for its moral attitudes. It is the genius of a Pirandello, a Brecht, or an Ionesco to cause such disturbance and by doing so to become genuine moral critics. Miller's limited theatre fits down inside the theatre of the world which the audience inhabits. His theatre is too small to touch the outer walls against which the genuinely objective drama would need to be played.

This point is made very clear in certain remarks he makes about *Death of a Salesman,* especially as we compare them with the confusion which lurks in every corner of that play. The following passage occurs in a discussion of Willy Loman's stature as a tragic figure:

> How can we respect a man who goes to such extremities over something he could in no way help or prevent? The answer, I think, is not that we respect the man, but that we respect the Law he has so completely broken, wittingly or not, for it is that Law which, we believe, defines us as men. The confusion of some critics viewing *Death of a Salesman* in this regard is that they do not see that Willy Loman has broken a law without whose protection life is insupportable if not incomprehensible to him and to many others; it is the law which says that a failure in society and in business has no right to live. Unlike the law against incest, the law of success is not administered by statute or church, but it is very nearly as powerful in its grip upon men. The confusion increases because, while it is a law, it is by no means a wholly agreeable one even as it is slavishly obeyed, for to fail is no longer to belong to society, in his estimate.

The confusion, I am afraid, lies not with the critics but with the playwright, and it is a very illustrative one. There is, in fact, no "law which says that a failure in society and in business has no right to live." It would, indeed, suit Miller's polemic better if there were. There is a *delusion* that a failure in society and in business has no right to live. To some people, such as Willy Loman, it may indeed seem like a law. But it is one thing for a character in a play to act as if something were a law, and quite another thing for the playwright to believe it. Miller's subsequent remarks in this same section of his essay make it perfectly clear that he himself, the audience, and also Willy Loman, do as a matter of fact have criteria according to which they suspect that this "law" is a hoax. It is in fact not a law but a false *credo*, which Willy shares with many persons, and the result of the attempt to make a false *credo* into a law results only in pathetic irony.

What is it, one wonders, that prevents Miller from probing Willy's consciousness and ours to the point of finding the truly objective world in which we still, in fact, believe and according to which Willy's "law" strikes us as so pathetic? If we ask where in the play one touches bedrock, the answer is nowhere. Is the law of success *really* a law? No. Miller tells us that "the system of love," which is "embodied in Biff Loman" was meant to counter Willy's "law." But if that is true, it was unfortunately not dramatized. That is, the way in which Biff's "law" of love judges and invalidates Willy's "law" of success is not revealed, and so the one is not actually a truth which is being brought to bear dramatically on the other.

The same ambiguity is seen in the question of society versus the individual. John Gassner said long ago that Arthur Miller had "split his play between *social causation* and *individual responsibility* for Willy's fate."[1] Is Willy's "law" the result of some defect in himself? If so, what is the nature of this defect, and what genuine law does it confound? Or is his "law" imposed upon him by a white-collar industrial society? If so, what is wrong with such a society and what truth does it prevent Willy Loman from seeing? Miller would probably resist making a decision in favor of either the individual or the social causation, and rightly so. But in that case, if he is interested in theatre worth the name of art, he has an obligation to examine his complex situation until the roots of Willy's anxiety are exposed, an exposure which would cause us to know something about the reality in which we are, if only unconsciously, living. It is in the lack of penetration into the objective philosophical situation that Miller fails us, with the result that we must settle for no more enlightenment upon our situation than pathetic Willy had upon his.

Miller deplores the loss of a "universal moral sanction," but he does nothing toward the discovery of a conceivable basis for one. In that respect he is, perhaps, no different from the majority of his contemporaries. It is not a surprising result, however, that he falls so easily into preaching and scolding his audience. (In his essay in the *Collected Plays* he is not above reproving those who staged or acted his plays, an attitude which reflects credit upon no one, least of all the playwright.) Miller's strident moralism is a good example of what happens when ideals must be maintained in an atmosphere of humanistic relativism. There being no objective good and evil, and no imperative other than conscience, man

[1] *The Theatre in Our Times,* New York, 1954, p. 347. Author's italics.

himself must be made to bear the full burden of creating his values and living up to them. The immensity of this task is beyond human capacity, even that of genius. To insist upon it without reference to ultimate truth is to create a situation productive of despair. This point has been seen by many writers of our day, but not by the liberal optimists, of which Miller is one. Here we have come to the second weakness which inevitably robs his work of stature.

At the time that *The Crucible* opened, Eric Bentley categorized Arthur Miller as an unreconstructed liberal and said that he "is the playwright of American liberal folklore."[2] The trouble with the play, he went on, was that it too neatly divided the sheep from the goats. "The guilty men are as black with guilt as Mr. Miller says — what we must ask is whether the innocent are as white with innocence." Mr. Bentley's remarks become all the more interesting when they are remembered in connection with a passage in the introduction to the *Collected Plays,* in which Miller describes his discovery, while writing *The Crucible,* of certain facts about human nature:

> I believe now, as I did not conceive then, that there are people dedicated to evil in the world; that without their perverse example we should not know the good. Evil is not a mistake but a fact in itself . . . I believe merely that, from whatever cause, a dedication to evil, not mistaking it for good, but knowing it as evil and loving it as evil, is possible in human beings who appear agreeable and normal. I think now that one of the hidden weaknesses of our whole approach to dramatic psychology is our inability to face this fact — to conceive, in effect, of Iago.

So far, we are on fairly safe ground, although we must note already that only certain people are dedicated to evil, others presumably going clean. But note how contradictory are the following sentiments. They are from the very same passage, in the place indicated above by the ellipsis:

> I have never proceeded psychoanalytically in my thought, but neither have I been separated from that humane if not humanistic conception of man as being essentially innocent while the evil in him represents but a perversion of his frustrated love. I posit no metaphysical force of evil which totally possesses certain individuals, nor do I even deny that given infinite wisdom and patience and knowledge any human being can be saved from himself.

Here the contradictory and self-limiting sentiments pass clearly before us. Evil is a fact, yet it is only a perversion of frustrated love. It is as absolute as in Iago, yet it may be cured with wisdom, patience, and knowledge. It is outside one's self and may be loved, yet it is only from himself that man needs to be saved. The passage reveals a head-on collision between illusions of human goodness and the facts of dedication to evil. Here we reach the straits through which the Miller realism will not pass.

No wonder *Death of a Salesman* cannot make up its mind whether the trouble is in Willy or in society. No wonder Willy is at one moment the pathetic object of our pity and the next is being defended as a hero of tragic dimensions. Miller is a playwright who wants morality without bothering to speak of a good in the light of which morality would make sense. On the one hand he wants a universal moral sanction; on the other he considers man's potentialities and limitations to lie entirely within himself. Out of such unresolved contradictions irony and pathos are the most we can get, and we are lucky to get those.

The concluding sentence of the essay we have been considering reads as follows:

> If there is one unseen goal toward which every play in this book strives, it is that very discovery and its proof — that we are made and yet are more than what made us.

I take this to mean that man transcends his hereditary and environmental situation. Well and good. But if we are to be able to speak of "moral sanctions" in drama or society, we must come to acknowledge that man is himself transcended by some truth that is not irrelevant to morality. Miller seems to flinch before that assertive act of the imagination which uncovers (or, in religious language, receives) the ontological ground upon which the truly meaningful act must stand. This is a level of the real which Miller has not yet explored, although it is the level demanded of one who would break out of the confusions that enveloped Willy Loman.

mary m<small>c</small>carthy

THE AMERICAN REALIST
PLAYWRIGHTS

As soon as this title is announced for a lecture or an article, a question pops up: Who are they? Is there, as is assumed abroad, a school of realists in the American theatre or is this notion a critical figment? The question is legitimate and will remain, I hope, in the air long after I have finished. Nevertheless, for purposes of discussion, I am going to take for granted that there is such a group, if not a school, and name its members: Arthur Miller, Tennessee Williams, William Inge, Paddy Chayevsky, the Elmer Rice of *Street Scene*.

Behind them, casting them in the shadow, stands the great figure of O'Neill, and opposite them, making them seem more homogeneous, are writers like George Kelly, Wilder, Odets, Saroyan. Their counterparts in the novel are Dreiser, Sherwood Anderson, James T. Farrell, the early Thomas Wolfe — which illustrates, by the way, the backwardness of the theatre in comparison with the novel. The theatre seems to be chronically twenty years behind, regardless of realism, as the relation of Beckett to Joyce, for example, shows. The theatre feeds on the novel; never *vice versa:* think of the hundreds of dramatisations of novels, and then try to think of a book that was "novelised" from a play. There is not even a word for it. The only actual case I can call to mind is *The Other House* by Henry James — a minor novel he salvaged from a play of his own that failed. To return, one characteristic of American realism in the theatre is that none of its practitioners currently — except Chayevsky — wants to call himself a realist. Tennessee Williams is known to his admirers as a "poetic realist," while Arthur Miller declares that he is an exponent of the "social play" and identifies himself with the Greek playwrights, whom he describes as social playwrights also. This delusion was dramatised, if that is the word, in *A View from the Bridge*.

The fact that hardly a one of these playwrights cares to be regarded as a realist without some qualifying or mitigating adjective being attached to the term invites a definition of realism. What does it mean in common parlance? I have looked the word *realist* up in the Oxford English Dictionary.

Reprinted from *Theatre Chronicles 1937–1962* by Mary McCarthy, by permission of Farrar, Straus & Giroux, Inc. Copyright © 1961 by Mary McCarthy.

. . . In reference to art and literature, sometimes used as a term of com-
mendation, when precision and vividness of detail are regarded as a merit,
and sometimes unfavourably contrasted with idealised description or representation. In recent use it has often been used with the implication that the
details are of an unpleasant or sordid character.

This strikes me as a very fair account of the historical fate of the notion
of realism, but I shall try to particularise a little, in the hope of finding
out why and how this happened. And I shall not be condemning realism
but only noting what people seem to think of it.

When we say that a novel or a play is realistic, we mean, certainly,
that it gives a picture of ordinary life. Its characters will be drawn from
the middle class, the lower middle class, occasionally the working class.
You cannot write realistic drama about upper-class life; at least, no one
ever has. Aristocracy does not lend itself to realistic treatment, but to
one or another kind of stylisation: romantic drama, romantic comedy,
comedy of manners, satire, tragedy. This fact in itself is a realistic criticism of the aristocratic idea, which cannot afford, apparently, to live in
the glass house of the realistic stage. Kings and noble men, said Aristotle,
are the protagonists of tragedy — not women or slaves. The same is true
of nobility of character or intellect. The exceptional man, whether he be
Oedipus or King Lear or one of the romantic revolutionary heroes of
Hugo or Musset, is fitted to be the protagonist of a tragedy, but just this
tragic fitness disqualifies him from taking a leading role in a realist
drama. Such figures as Othello or Hernani can never be the subject of
realistic treatment, unless it is with the object of deflating them, showing
how *ordinary* — petty or squalid — they are. But then the hero is no
longer Othello but an imposter posing as Othello. Cut down to size, he
is just like everybody else but worse, because he is a fraud into the
bargain.

This abrupt foreshortening is why realistic treatment of upper-class
life always takes the harsh plunge into satire. No man is a hero to his
valet, and Beaumarchais' Figaro is the spokesman of social satire — not
of realism; his personal and private realism turns his master into a clown.
Realism deals with ordinary men and women or, in extreme forms, with
subordinary men, men on the level of beasts or of blind conditioned
reflexes (*La Bête Humaine, The Hairy Ape*). This tendency is usually
identified with naturalism, but I am regarding naturalism as simply a
variety of realism.

Realism, historically, is associated with two relatively modern inventions, *i.e.*, with journalism and with photography. "Photographic realism"
is a pejorative term, and enemies of realistic literature often dismissed it
as "no more than journalism," implying that journalism was a sordid,
seamy affair — a daily photographic close-up, as it were, of the clogged

pores of society. The author as sheer observer likened himself to a camera (Dos Passos, Christopher Isherwood, Wright Morris), and in so far as the realistic novel was vowed to be a reflector of ordinary life, the newspapers inevitably became a prime source of material. Newspaper accounts impressed the 19th century with their quality of "stark objectivity," and newspapers, which appeared every day, seemed to be the repositories of everydayness and to give a multiple image of the little tragedies and vicissitudes of daily life. In America, in the early part of this century, the realistic novel was a partner of what was called "muckraking" journalism, and both were linked with populism and crusades for political reform.

Hence, perhaps, in part, the unsavoury associations in common speech of the word *realistic*, even when applied in non-literary contexts. Take the phrase "a realistic decision." If someone tells you he is going to make "a realistic decision," you immediately understand that he has resolved to do something bad. The same with *Realpolitik*. A "realistic politics" is a euphemism for a politics of harsh opportunism; if you hear someone say that it is time for a government to follow a realistic line, you can interpret that as meaning that it is time for principles to be abandoned. A politician or a political thinker who calls himself a realist is usually boasting that he sees politics, so to speak, in the raw; he is generally a proclaimed cynic and pessimist who makes it his business to look behind words and fine speeches for the motive. This motive is always low.

Whatever the field, whenever you hear that a subject is to be treated "realistically," you expect that its unpleasant aspects are to be brought forward. So it is with the play and the novel. A delicate play like Turgenev's *A Month in the Country*, though perfectly truthful to life, seems deficient in realism in comparison with the stronger medicine of Gorki's *The Lower Depths*. This is true of Turgenev's novels as well and of such English writers as Mrs. Gaskell. And of the peaceful parts of *War and Peace*. Ordinary life treated in its uneventful aspects tends to turn into an idyll. We think of Turgenev and Mrs. Gaskell almost as pastoral writers, despite the fact that their faithful sketches have nothing in common with the artificial convention of the true pastoral. We suspect that there is something arcadian here — something "unrealistic."

If realism deals with the ordinary man embedded in ordinary life, which for the most part is uneventful, what then is the criterion that makes us forget Turgenev or Mrs. Gaskell when we name off the realists? I think it is this: what we call realism, and particularly dramatic realism, tends to single out the ordinary man at the moment he might get into the newspaper. The criterion, in other words, is drawn from journalism. The ordinary man must become "news" before he qualifies to be the protagonist of a realistic play or novel. The exceptional man is news at all times, but how can the ordinary man get into the paper? By committing a crime. Or, more rarely, by getting involved in a spectacular accident. Since accidents, in general, are barred from the drama, this leaves crime — murder or suicide or embezzlement. And we find that the protagonists of realistic drama, by and large, are the protagonists of newspaper stories—"little men" who have shot their wives or killed themselves in the garage or gone to jail for fraud or embezzlement.

Now drama has always had an affinity for crime; long before realism was known, Oedipus and Clytemnestra and Macbeth and Othello were famous for their deeds of blood. But the crimes of tragedy are the crimes of heroes, while the crimes of realistic drama are the crimes of the nondescript person, the crimes that are, in a sense, all alike. The individual in the realistic drama is regarded as a cog or a statistic; he commits the uniform crime that sociologically he might be expected to commit. That is, supposing that 1,031 bookkeepers in the State of New York are destined to tamper with the accounts, and 304 policemen are destined to shoot their wives, and 1,115 householders to do away with themselves in the garage, each individual bookkeeper, cop, and householder has been holding a ticket in this statistical lottery, like the fourteen Athenian youths and maidens sent off yearly to the Minotaur's labyrinth, and he acquires interest for the realist theatre only when his "number" comes up. To put it as simply as possible, the cop in *Street Scene* commits his crime — wife-murder — without having the moral freedom to choose to commit it, just as Willy Loman in *Death of a Salesman* commits suicide — under sociological pressure.

The hero of tragedy, on the contrary, is a morally free being who identifies himself with his crime (*i.e.*, elects it), and this is true even where he is fated, like Oedipus, to commit it and can be said to have no personal choice in the matter. Oedipus both rejects and accepts his deeds, embraces them in free will at last as *his*. It is the same with Othello or Hamlet. The distinction will be clear if you ask yourself what tragedy of Shakespeare is closest to the realistic theatre. The answer, surely, is *Macbeth*. And why? Because of Lady Macbeth. Macbeth really doesn't choose to murder the sleeping Duncan; Lady Macbeth chooses for him; he is like a middle-aged husband, nagged on by his ambitious wife, the way the second vice-president of a bank is nagged on by his Mrs. Macbeth, who wants him to become first vice-president. The end of the tragedy, however, reverses all this; Macbeth becomes a hero only late in the drama, when he pushes Lady Macbeth aside and takes all his deeds on himself. Paradoxically, the conspicuous tragic hero is never free *not* to do his deed; he cannot escape it, as Hamlet found. But the mute hero or protagonist of a realistic play is always free, at least seemingly, not to emerge from obscurity and get his picture in the paper. There is always the chance that not he but some other non-descript bookkeeper or policeman will answer the statistical call.

The heroes of realistic plays are clerks, bookkeepers, policemen, housewives, salesmen, schoolteachers, small and middling business men. They commit crimes but they cannot be professional criminals (unlike the heroes of Genêt or the characters in *The Beggars' Opera*), for professional criminals, like kings and noblemen, are a race apart. The settings of realistic plays are offices, drab dining-rooms or living-rooms, or the backyard, which might be defined as a place where some grass has once been planted and failed to grow.

The backyard is a favorite locus for American realist plays, but no realist play takes place in a garden. Nature is excluded from the realist play, as it has been from the realistic novel. The presence of Nature in Turgenev (and in Chekhov) denotes, as I have suggested, a pastoral intrusion. If a realist play does not take place in the backyard, where Nature has been eroded by clothes-poles, garbage cans, bottled-gas tanks, and so on, it takes place indoors, where the only plant, generally, is a rubber-plant. Even with Ibsen, the action is confined to a room or pair of rooms until the late plays like *A Lady from the Sea, The Master Builder, John Gabriel Borkman,* when the realistic style has been abandoned for symbolism and the doors are swung open to the garden, mountains, the sea. Ibsen, however, is an exception to the general rule that the indoor scene must be unattractive: his middle-class Scandinavians own handsome furniture; Nora's house, like any doll's house, must have been charmingly appointed. But Ibsen is an exception to another rule that seems to govern realistic drama (and the novel too, for that matter) — the rule that it must not be well written. (Thanks to William Archer's wooden translations, his work now falls into line in English.) This rule in America has the force, almost, of a law, one of those iron laws that work from within necessity itself, apparently, and without conscious human aid. Our American realists do not *try* to write badly. Many, like Arthur Miller, strive to write "well," *i.e.*, pretentiously, but like Dreiser in the novel they are cursed with inarticulateness. They "grope." They are, as O'Neill said of himself, "fogbound."

The heroes are petty or colourless; the settings are drab; the language is lame. Thus the ugliness of the form is complete. I am not saying this as a criticism, only observing that when a play or a novel fails to meet these norms, we cease to think of it as realistic. Flaubert, known to be a "stylist," ceases to count for us as a realist, and even in the last century, Matthew Arnold, hailing Tolstoy as a realist, was blinded by categorical thinking — with perhaps a little help from the translations — into calling his novels raw "slices of life," sprawling, formless, and so on. But it is these clichés, in the long run, that have won out. The realistic novel today is more like what Arnold thought Tolstoy was than it is like Tolstoy or any of the early realists.

This question of the beauty of form also touches the actor. An actor formerly was supposed to be a good-looking man, with a handsome figure, beautiful movements, and a noble diction. These attributes are no longer necessary for a stage career; indeed, in America they are a positive handicap. A good-looking young man who moves well and speaks well is becoming almost unemployable in American "legit" theatre; his best hope to-day is to look for work in musical comedy. Or posing for advertisements. On the English stage, where realism until recently never got a foothold, the good-looking actor still rules the roost, but the English actor cannot play American realist parts, while the American actor cannot play Shakespeare or Shaw. A pretty girl in America may still hope to be an actress, though even here there are signs of a change: the heroine of O'Neill's late play, *A Moon for the Misbegotten,* was a freckled giantess five feet eleven inches tall and weighing 180 pounds.

Eisenstein and the Italian neo-realists used people off the streets for actors — a logical inference from premises which, being egalitarian and documentary, are essentially hostile to professional élites, including Cossacks, Swiss Guards, and actors. The professional actor in his greasepaint is the antithesis of the pallid man on the street. But film and stage realism are not so democratic in their principles as may first appear.

To begin with, the director and a small corps of professionals — electricians and camera men — assume absolute power over the masses, *i.e.,* over the untrained actors picked from the crowd; no resistance is encountered, as it would be with professional actors, in moulding the human material to the director-dictator's will. And even with stars and all-professional casts, the same tendency is found in the modern realist or neo-realist director. Hence the whispered stories of film stars deliberately broken by a director: James Dean and Brigitte Bardot. Similar stories of brain-washing are heard back-stage. This is not surprising if realism, as we now know it, rejects as non-average whatever is noble, beautiful, or seemly, whatever is capable of "gesture," whatever, in fact, is free.

Everything I have been saying up till now can be summed up in a sentence. Realism is a depreciation of the real. It is a gloomy puritan doctrine that has flourished chiefly in puritan countries — America, Ireland, Scandinavia, northern France, non-conformist England — chilly, chillblained countries, where the daily world is ugly and everything is done to keep it so, as if a punishment for sin. The doctrine is spreading with industrialisation, the growth of ugly cities, and the erosion of Nature. It came late to the English stage, long after it had appeared in

the novel, because those puritan elements with which it naturally allied
have, up until now, considered the theatre to be wicked.

At the same time, in defence of realism, it must be said that its great
enemy has been just that puritan life whose colour it has taken. The
original realists — Ibsen in the theatre, Flaubert in the novel — regarded
themselves as "pagans," in opposition to their puritan contemporaries,
and adhered to a religion of Beauty or Nature; they dreamed of freedom
and hedonistic licence (Flaubert) and exalted (Ibsen) the autonomy of
the individual will. Much of this "paganism" is still found in O'Casey
and in the early O'Neill, a curdled puritan of Irish-American stock. The
original realists were half-Dionysian aesthetes ("The vine-leaves in his
hair") and their heroes and heroines were usually rebels, protesting the
drabness and meanness of the common life. Ibsen's characters complain
that they are "stifling;" in the airless hypocrisy of the puritan middle-
class parlour, people were being poisoned by the dead gas of lies. Hypocrisy is the cardinal sin of the middle class, and the exposure of a lie
is at the centre of all Ibsen's plots.

The strength and passion of realism is its resolve to tell the whole
truth; this explains why the realist in his indictment of society avoids
the old method of satire with its delighted exaggeration. The realist
drama at its highest is an implacable exposé. Ibsen rips off the curtain
and shows his audiences to themselves, and there is something inescapable in the manner of the confrontation, like a case slowly being built.
The pillars of society who sit in the best seats are, bit by bit, informed
that they are rotten and that the commerce they live on is a commerce
of "coffin ships." The action on the Ibsen stage is too close for comfort
to the lives of the audience; only the invisible "fourth wall" divides
them. "This is the way we live now!" — moral examination, self-exter-
mination, are practised as a duty, a protestant stocktaking in the realist
mission hall.

For this, it is essential that the audience accept the picture as true;
it cannot be permitted to feel that it is watching something "made up"
or embellished. Hence the stripping down of the form and the elimination of effects that might be recognised as literary. For the first time too,
in the realist drama, the accessories of the action are described at length
by the playwright. The details must strike home and convince. The
audience must be able to place the furniture, the carpets, the ornaments,
the napery and glassware as "just what these people would have." This
accounts for the importance of the stage set. Many critics who scornfully
dismiss the "boxlike set" of the realistic drama, with its careful disposition
of furniture, do not understand its function. This box is the box or
"coffin" of average middle-class life opened at one end to reveal the
corpse within, looking, as all embalmed corpses are said to do, "just as if

it were alive." Inside the realist drama, whenever it is genuine and serious, there is a kind of double illusion, a false bottom: everything appears
to be lifelike but this appearance of life is death. The stage set remains
a central element in all true realism; it cannot be replaced by scrim or
platforms.

In *Long Day's Journey into Night,* surely the greatest realist drama
since Ibsen, the family living-room, with its central overhead lighting-
fixture is as solid and eternal as oak and as sad as wicker, and O'Neill in
the text tells the stage-designer what books must be in the glassed-in
bookcase on the left and what books in the other by the entrance. The
tenement of Elmer Rice's *Street Scene* (in the opera version) was a
magnificent piece of characterisation; so was the Bronx living-room of
Odets' *Awake and Sing* — his sole (and successful) experiment with realism. I can still see the bowl of fruit on the table, slightly to the left of
stage centre, and hear the Jewish mother interrupting whoever happened
to be talking, to say, "Have a piece of fruit." That bowl of fruit, which
was the Jewish Bronx, remains more memorable as a character than many
of the people in the drama. This gift of characterisation through props
and stage set is shared by Paddy Chayevsky in *In the Middle of the Night*
and by William Inge in *Come Back, Little Sheba,* where an unseen prop
or accessory, the housewife's terrible frowsty little dog, is a master-stroke
of realist illusion and, more than that, a kind of ghostly totem. All these
plays, incidentally, are stories of death-in-life.

This urgent correspondence with a familiar reality, down to the last
circumstantial detail, is what makes realism so gripping, like a trial in
court. The dramatist is witnessing or testifying, on an oath never sworn
before in a work of art, not to leave out anything and to tell the truth to
the best of his ability. And yet the realistic dramatist, beginning with
Ibsen, is aware of a missing element. The realist mode seems to generate
a dissatisfaction with itself, even in the greatest masters: Tolstoy, for
example, came to feel that his novels, up to *Resurrection,* were inconse-
quential trifling; the vital truth had been left out. In short, as a novelist,
he began to feel like a hypocrite. This dissatisfaction with realism was
evidently suffered also by Ibsen; half-way through his realist period, you
see him start to look for another dimension. Hardly had he discovered
or invented the new dramatic mode than he showed signs of being
cramped by it; he experienced, if his plays are an index, that same sense
of confinement, of being stifled, within the walls of realism that his
characters experience within the walls of middle-class life. Something
was missing: air.

This is already plain in *The Wild Duck,* a strange piece of auto-
criticism and probably his finest play; chafing, restless, mordant, he is
searching for something else, for a poetic element, which he represents,

finally, in the wild duck itself, a dramatic symbol for that cherished wild freedom that neither Ibsen nor his characters can maintain, without harming it, in a shut-in space. But to resort to symbols to make good the missing element becomes a kind of forcing, like trying to raise a wild bird in an attic, and the strain of this is felt in *Rosmersholm,* where symbols play a larger part and are charged with a more oppressive weight of meaning. In *The Lady from the Sea, The Master Builder,* and other late plays, the symbols have broken through the thin fence or framework of realism; poetry has spread its crippled wings, but the price has been heavy.

The whole history of dramatic realism is encapsulated in Ibsen. First, the renunciation of verse and of historical and philosophical subjects in the interests of prose and the present time; then the dissatisfaction and the attempt to restore the lost element through a recourse to symbols; then, or at the same time, a forcing of the action of the climaxes to heighten the drama; finally, the renunciation of realism in favour of a mixed mode or hodge-podge.

The reaching for tragedy at the climaxes is evident in *Hedda Gabler* and still more so in *Rosmersholm,* where, to me at any rate, that climactic shriek "To the mill race!" is absurdly like a bad film. Many of Ibsen's big moments, even as early as *The Doll's House,* strike me as false and grandiose, that is, precisely, as stagey. Nor is it only in the context of realism that they appear so. It is not just that one objects that people do not act or talk like that — Tolstoy's criticism of King Lear on the heath. If you compare the mill-race scene in *Rosmersholm* with the climax of a Shakespearean tragedy, you will see that the Shakespearean heroes are far less histrionic, more natural and *ordinary;* there is always a stillness at the centre of the Shakespearean storm. It is as if the realist, in reaching for tragedy, were punished for his *hubris* by a ludicrous fall into bathos. Tragedy is impossible by definition in the quotidian realist mode, since (quite aside from the question of the hero) tragedy is the exceptional action, one of whose signs is beauty.

In America the desire to supply the missing element (usually identified as poetry or "beauty") seems to grow stronger and stronger exactly in proportion to the author's awkwardness with language. The less a playwright can write prose, the more he wishes to write poetry and to raise his plays by their bootstraps to a higher realm.

You find these applications of "beauty" in Arthur Miller and Tennessee Williams; they stand out like rouge on a pitted complexion; it is as though the author first wrote the play naturalistically and then gave it a beauty-treatment or face-lift. Before them, O'Neill, who was too honest and too philosophically inclined to be satisfied by a surface solution, kept looking methodically for a way of representing the missing element in dramas that would still be realistic at the core. He experimented with masks (*The Great God Brown*), with the aside and the soliloquy (*Strange Interlude*), with a story and pattern borrowed from Greek classic drama (*Mourning Becomes Electra*). In other words, he imported into the American home or farm the machinery of tragedy. But his purpose was always a greater realism. His use of the aside, for example, was very different from the traditional use of the aside (a kind of nudge to the audience, usually on the part of the villain, to let them in on his true intent or motive); in *Strange Interlude* O'Neill was trying, through the aside, to make available to the realistic drama the discoveries of modern psychology, to represent on the stage the unconscious selves of his characters, at cross-purposes with their conscious selves but just as real if not realer, at least according to the psycho-analysts. He was trying, in short, to give a more complete picture of ordinary people in their daily lives.

It was the same with his use of masks in *The Great God Brown;* he was appropriating the mask of Athenian drama, a ritual means of putting a distance between the human actor and the audience, to bring his own audience closer to the inner humanity of his character — the man behind the mask of conformity. The fact that these devices were clumsy is beside the point. O'Neill's sincerity usually involved him in clumsiness. In the end, he came back to the straight realism of his beginnings: *The Long Voyage Home,* the title of his young Caribbean series, could also be the title of the great play of his old age: *Long Day's Journey into Night.* He has sailed beyond the horizon and back into port; the circle is complete. In this late play, the quest for the missing element, as such, is renounced; poetry is held to be finally unattainable by the author.

"I couldn't touch what I tried to tell you just now," says the character who is supposed to be the young O'Neill. "I just stammered. That's the best I'll ever do. I mean, if I live. Well, it will be faithful realism, at least. Stammering is the native eloquence of us fog people."

In this brave acknowledgement or advance acceptance of failure, there is something very moving. Moreover, the acceptance of defeat was in fact the signal of a victory. *Long Day's Journey into Night,* sheer dogged prose from beginning to end, achieves in fact a peculiar poetry, and the relentless amassing of particulars takes on, eventually, some of the crushing force of inexorable logic that we find in Racine or in a Greek play. The weight of circumstances itself becomes a fate or nemesis. This is the closest, probably, that realism can get to tragedy.

The "stammering" of O'Neill was what made his later plays so long, and the stammering, which irritated some audiences, impatient for the next syllable to fall, was a sign of the author's agonised determination to be truthful. If O'Neill succeeded, at last, in deepening the character of his realism, it was because the missing element he strove to represent was not, in the end, "poetry" or "beauty" or "philosophy" (though he sometimes seems to have felt that it was) but simply meaning — the total significance of an action. What he came to conclude, rather wearily, in his last plays was that the total significance of an action lay in the accumulated minutiæ of that action and could not be abstracted from it, at least not by him. There was no truth or meaning beyond the event itself; anything more (or less) would be a lie. This pun or tautology, this conundrum, committed him to a cycle of repetition, and memory, the mother of the Muses, became his only muse.

The younger American playwrights — Miller, Williams, Inge, Chayevsky — now all middle-aged, are pledged, like O'Neill, to verisimilitude. They purport to offer a "slice of life," in Tennessee Williams' case a rich, spicy slab of Southern fruit cake, but still a slice of life. The locus of their plays is the American porch or backyard or living-room or parlour or bus station, presented as typical, authentic as home-fried potatoes or "real Vermont maple syrup." This authenticity may be regional, as with Williams and Paddy Chayevsky (the Jewish upper West side; a Brooklyn synagogue) or it may claim to be as broad as the nation, as with Arthur Miller, or somewhere rather central, in between the two, as with William Inge. But in any case, the promise of these playwrights is to show an ordinary home, an ordinary group of bus passengers, a typical manufacturer, and so on, and the *dramatis personæ* tend to resemble a small-town, non-blue-ribbon jury: housewife, lawyer, salesman, chiropractor, working-man, schoolteacher. . . .

Though Tennessee Williams' characters are more exotic, they too are offered as samples to the audience's somewhat voyeuristic eye; when Williams' film, *Baby Doll,* was attacked by Cardinal Spellman, the director (Elia Kazan) defended it on the grounds that it was true to the life that he and Williams had observed, on location, in Mississippi. If the people in Tennessee Williams were regarded as products of the author's imagination, his plays would lose all their interest. There is always a point in any one of Williams' dramas where recognition gives way to a feeling of shocked incredulity; this shock technique is the source of his sensational popularity. But the audience would not be electrified if it had not been persuaded earlier that it was witnessing something the author vouched for as a common, ordinary occurrence in the Deep South.

Unlike the other playwrights, who make a journalistic claim to neutral recording, Arthur Miller admittedly has a message. His first-produced play, *All My Sons,* was a social indictment taken, almost directly, from Ibsen's *Pillars of Society.* The coffin ships, rotten, unseaworthy vessels caulked over to give an appearance of soundness, become

defective airplanes sold to the government by a corner-cutting manufacturer during the Second World War; like the coffin ships, the airplanes are a symbol of the inner rottenness of bourgeois society, and the
sins of the father, as *almost* in Ibsen, are visited on the son, a pilot who
cracks up in the Pacific theatre (in Ibsen, the shipowner's boy is saved at
the last minute from sailing on *The Indian Girl*). The insistence of this
symbol and the vagueness or absence of concrete detail express Miller's
impatience with the particular and his feeling that his play ought to say
"more" than it appears to be saying. Ibsen, even in his later, symbolic
works, was always specific about the where, when, and how of his histories (the biographies of his central characters are related with almost
too much circumstantiality), but Miller has always regarded the specific
as trivial and has sought, from the very outset, a hollow, reverberant
universality.

The reluctance to awaken a specific recognition, for fear that a
larger meaning might go unrecognised by the public, grew on Miller
with *Death of a Salesman* — a strong and original conception that was
enfeebled by its creator's insistence on universality and by a too-hortatory
excitement, *i.e.*, an eagerness to preach, which is really another form of
the same thing. Miller was bent on making his Salesman (as he calls
him) a parable of Everyman, exactly as in a clergyman's sermon, so that
the drama has only the quality — and something of the canting tone —
of an illustrative moral example.

The thirst for universality becomes even more imperious in *A View
from the Bridge*, where the account of a waterfront killing that Miller read
in a newspaper is accessorised with Greek architecture, "archetypes,"
and, from time to time, intoned passages of verse; and Miller announces
in a preface that he is not interested in his hero's "psychology." Miller
does not understand that you cannot turn a newspaper item about
Italian longshoremen and illegal immigration into a Greek play by adding a chorus and the pediment of a temple. Throughout Miller's long
practice as a realist, there is not only a naïve searching for another
dimension but an evident hatred of and contempt for reality — as not
good enough to make plays out of.

It is natural, therefore, that he should never have had any interest
in how people talk; his characters all talk the same way — somewhat
funereally, through their noses. A live sense of speech differences (think
of Shaw's *Pygmalion*) is rare in American playwrights; O'Neill tried to
cultivate it ("dat ol davil sea"), but he could never do more than write
perfunctory dialect, rather like somebody telling a Pat and Mike story
or a mountaineer joke.

The only American realist with an ear for speech, aside from
Chayevsky, whose range is narrow, is Tennessee Williams. He does really

hear his characters, especially his female characters; he has studied their speech patterns and, like Professor Higgins, he can tell where they come from; Williams too is the only current realist who places his characters in social history. Of all the realists, after O'Neill, he has probably the greatest native gift for the theatre; he is a natural performer and comedian, and it is too bad that he suffers from the inferiority complex that is the curse of the recent American realists — the sense that a play must be bigger than its characters. This is really a social disease — a fear of being under-rated — rather than the claustrophobia of the medium itself, which tormented Ibsen and O'Neill.

But it goes back to the same source: the depreciation of the real. Real speech, for example, is not good enough for Williams and from time to time he silences his characters to put on a phonograph record of his special poetic longplay prose.

All dramatic realism is somewhat sadistic; an audience is persuaded to watch something that makes it uncomfortable and from which no relief is offered — no laughter, no tears, no purgation. This sadism had a moral justification, so long as there was the question of the exposure of a l'e. But Williams is fascinated by the refinements of cruelty, which with him becomes a form of æstheticism, and his plays, far from baring a lie that society is trying to cover up, titillate society like a peepshow. The curtain is ripped off, to disclose, not a drab scene of ordinary life, but a sadistic exhibition of the kind certain rather specialised tourists pay to see in big cities like New Orleans. With Williams, it is always a case of watching some mangy cat on a hot tin roof. The ungratified sexual organ of an old maid, a young wife married to a homosexual, a subnormal poor white farmer is proffered to the audience as a curiosity. The withholding of sexual gratification from a creature or "critter" in heat for three long acts is Williams' central device; other forms of torture to which these poor critters are subjected are hysterectomy and castration. Nobody, not even the S.P.C.A., would argue that it was a good thing to show the prolonged torture of a dumb animal on the stage, even though the torture were only simulated and animals, in the end, would profit from such cases being brought to light. Yet this, on a human level, is Tennessee Williams' realism — a cat, to repeat, on a hot tin roof.

And, in a milder version, it is found again in William Inge's *Picnic*. No one could have prophesied, a hundred years ago, that the moral doctrine of realism would narrow to the point of becoming pornography, yet something like that seems to be happening with such realistic novels as *Peyton Place* and the later John O'Hara and with one branch of the realist theatre.

Realism seems to be a highly unstable mode, attracted on the one hand to the higher, on the other to the lower elements in the human scale, tending always to proceed towards its opposite, that is, to irreality, tracing a vicious circle from which it can escape only by repudiating the question — the question of reality.

To find the ideal realist, you would first have to find reality. And if no dramatist to-day, except O'Neill, can accept being a realist in its full implications, this is perhaps because of lack of courage. Ibsen and O'Neill, with all their dissatisfaction, produced major works in the full realist vein; the recent realists get discouraged after a single effort. *Street Scene, All My Sons, The Glass Menagerie, Come Back, Little Sheba, In the Middle of the Night,* perhaps *Awake and Sing* are the only convincing evidence that exists of an American realist school — not counting O'Neill. If I add *Death of a Salesman* and *A Streetcar Named Desire,* it is only because I do not know where else to put them.

james a. herne

ART FOR TRUTH'S SAKE
IN THE DRAMA

"Art for art's sake" seems to me to concern itself principally with delicacy of touch, with skill. It is æsthetic. It emphasizes beauty. It aims to be attractive. It must always be beautiful. It must contain no distasteful quality. It never offends. It is high-bred, so to speak. It holds that truth is ugly, or at least is not always beautiful. The compensation of the artist is the joy of having produced it.

"Art for truth's sake," on the other hand, emphasizes humanity. It is not sufficient that the subject be attractive or beautiful, or that it does not offend. It must first of all express some *large* truth. That is to say, it must always be representative. Truth is not always beautiful, but in art for truth's sake it is indispensable.

Art for art's sake may be likened to the exquisite decoration of some noble building; while art for truth's sake might be the building itself.

Art for truth's sake is serious. Its highest purpose has ever been

From James A. Herne, "Art for Truth's Sake in the Drama," *Arena,* XVII (February, 1897), 361–370.

to perpetuate the life of its time. The higher the form of expression the greater the art. . . .

I stand for art for truth's sake because it perpetuates the everyday life of its time, because it develops the latent beauty of the so-called commonplaces of life, because it dignifies labor and reveals the divinity of the common man.

It is generally held that the province of the drama is to amuse. I claim that it has a higher purpose — that its mission is to interest and to instruct. It should not *preach* objectively, but it should teach subjectively; and so I stand for truth in the drama, because it is elemental, it gets to the bottom of a question. It strikes at unequal standards and unjust systems. It is as unyielding as it is honest. It is as tender as it is inflexible. It has supreme faith in man. It believes that that which was good in the beginning cannot be bad at the end. It sets forth clearly that the concern of one is the concern of all. It stands for the higher development and thus the individual liberty of the human race.

owen davis

WHY I QUIT WRITING MELODRAMA

[*A master of the vivid and violent melodrama at the turn of the century tells how these plays were written.*]

The plays that we produced were written largely by rule. In fact the actual writing of one of these sensational melodramas I had reduced to a formula, about as follows:

TITLE (at least fifty per cent of success)
PLOT: Brief story of the play.
CAST: *Leading Man,* very (even painfully) virtuous.
  Leading Woman, in love with him.
  Comedy Man, always faithful friend of *Hero.*
  Soubrette, very worthy person (poor but honest) and always in love with
    Comedian.

From Owen Davis, "Why I Quit Writing Melodrama," *American Magazine,* LXXVIII (September, 1914), 28–31. Reprinted by permission of Donald Davis.

Heavy Man, a villain, not for any special reason, but, like "Topsy," "born bad."

Heavy Woman, — here I had a wider choice, his lady being allowed to fasten her affections upon either *Hero* or *Villain* (sometimes both) but never happily.

Father (or *Mother*), to provide sentiment.

Fill in as desired with character parts.

Aст I — Start the trouble.

Aст II — Here things look bad. The lady having left home, is quite at the mercy of *Villain.*

Aст III — The lady is saved by the help of the Stage Carpenter. (The big scenic and mechanical effects were always in Act III.)

Aст IV — The lovers are united and the villains are punished.

I suppose that I have been responsible for as many executions as the Queen in "Alice in Wonderland." I am honest enough to admit my cold-blooded attitude; but apply this chart to many plays of authors who consider their work inspired, and see if it fits.

These plays depended very greatly upon scenic effect, sensational dramatic title, and enormously melodramatic pictorial display on the bill boards. I think we touched upon every theme known to man, and every location. We limited ourselves, however, to American subjects. We always had a clear and dominant love interest, which we crossed with an element of danger, usually furnished by a rather impossible villain or adventuress. The themes of some of these plays were absolutely legitimate and the stories in many cases, with different dressing, would have done for a Broadway theater of the present day. But we had to, or fancied we had to, have such an overabundance of climactic material that our plays resulted in an undigested mass of unprepared situations. Where one carefully prepared and well-developed episode would really have been of far greater dramatic value, we made a rule of dividing our plays into no less than fifteen scenes, the end of each being a moment of perilous suspense or terrifying danger. This gave the playwright rather less than seven minutes to instruct his audience, to prepare his climaxes, to plant the seed for the next scene, and to *reach* his climaxes, which of course was absurdly impossible and resulted, I feel sure, in a form of entertainment which was only too ready to yield to the encroachment of the cheap vaudeville and moving pictures.

eugene o'neill

AN EXPLANATION OF
THE GREAT GOD BROWN

I realize that when a playwright takes to explaining he thereby automatically places himself "in the dock." But where an open-faced avowal by the play itself of the abstract theme underlying it is made impossible by the very nature of that hidden theme, then perhaps it is justifiable for the author to confess the mystical pattern which manifests itself as an overtone in *The Great God Brown*, dimly behind and beyond the words and actions of the characters.

I had hoped the names chosen for my people would give a strong hint of this. (An old scheme, admitted — Shakespeare and multitudes since.) Dion Anthony — Dionysus and St. Anthony — the creative pagan acceptance of life, fighting eternal war with the masochistic, life-denying spirit of Christianity as represented by St. Anthony — the whole struggle resulting in this modern day in mutual exhaustion — creative joy in life for life's sake frustrated, rendered abortive, distorted by morality from Pan into Satan, into a Mephistopheles mocking himself in order to feel alive; Christianity, once heroic in martyrs for its intense faith now pleading weakly for intense belief in anything, even Godhead itself. (In the play it is Cybele, the pagan Earth Mother, who makes the assertion with authority: "Our Father, Who Art!" to the dying Brown, as it is she who tries to inspire Dion Anthony with her certainty in life for its own sake.)

Margaret is my image of the modern direct descendant of the Marguerite of Faust — the eternal girl-woman with a virtuous simplicity of instinct, properly oblivious to everything but the means to her end of maintaining the race.

Cybel is an incarnation of Cybele, the Earth Mother doomed to segregation as a pariah in a world of unnatural laws, but patronized by her segregators, who are thus themselves the first victims of their laws.

Brown is the visionless demi-god of our new materialistic myth — a Success — building his life of exterior things, inwardly empty and resourceless, an uncreative creature of superficial preordained social grooves, a by-product forced aside into slack waters by the deep main current of life-desire.

From the New York *Evening Post*, February 13, 1926. Reproduced by Courtesy of the New York *Post*.

Dion's mask of Pan which he puts on as a boy is not only a defense against the world for the supersensitive painter-poet underneath it, but also an integral part of his character as the artist. The world is not only blind to the man beneath, but it also sneers at and condemns the Pan-mask it sees. After that Dion's inner self retrogresses along the line of Christian resignation until it partakes of the nature of the Saint while at the same time the outer Pan is slowly transformed by his struggle with reality into Mephistopheles. It is as Mephistopheles he falls stricken at Brown's feet after having condemned Brown to destruction by willing him his mask, but, this mask falling off as he dies, it is the Saint who kisses Brown's feet in abject contrition and pleads as a little boy to a big brother to tell him a prayer.

Brown has always envied the creative life force in Dion — what he himself lacks. When he steals Dion's mask of Mephistopheles he thinks he is gaining the power to live creatively, while in reality he is only stealing that creative power made self-destructive by complete frustration. This devil of mocking doubt makes short work of him. It enters him, rending him apart, torturing and transfiguring him until he is even forced to wear a mask of his Success, William A. Brown, before the world, as well as Dion's mask toward wife and children. Thus Billy Brown becomes not himself to anyone. And thus he partakes of Dion's anguish — more poignantly, for Dion has the Mother, Cybele — and in the end out of this anguish his soul is born, a tortured Christian soul such as the dying Dion's, begging for belief, and at the last finding it on the lips of Cybel.

And now for an explanation regarding this explanation. It was far from my idea in writing *Brown* that this background pattern of conflicting tides in the soul of Man should ever overshadow and thus throw out of proportion the living drama of the recognizable human beings, Dion, Brown, Margaret and Cybel. I meant it always to be mystically within and behind them, giving them a significance beyond themselves, forcing itself through them to expression in mysterious words, symbols, actions they do not themselves comprehend. And that is as clearly as I wish an audience to comprehend it. It is Mystery — the mystery any one man or woman can feel but not understand as the meaning of any event — or accident — in any life on earth. And it is this mystery I want to realize in the theater. The solution, if there ever be any, will probably have to be produced in a test tube and turn out to be discouragingly undramatic.

maxwell anderson

THE ESSENCE OF TRAGEDY

Anybody who dares to discuss the making of tragedy lays himself
open to critical assault and general barrage, for the theorists have been
hunting for the essence of tragedy since Aristotle without entire success.
There is no doubt that playwrights have occasionally written tragedy
successfully, from Aeschylus on, and there is no doubt that Aristotle came
very close to a definition of what tragedy is in his famous passage on
catharsis. But why the performance of tragedy should have a cleansing
effect on the audience, why an audience is willing to listen to tragedy,
why tragedy has a place in the education of men, has never, to my knowledge, been convincingly stated. I must begin by saying that I have not
solved the Sphinx's riddle which fifty generations of skillful brains have
left in shadow. But I have one suggestion which I think might lead to a
solution if it were put to laboratory tests by those who know something
about philosophical analysis and dialectic.

There seems no way to get at this suggestion except through a
reference to my own adventures in playwriting, so I ask your tolerance
while I use myself as an instance. A man who has written successful
plays is usually supposed to know something about the theory of playwriting, and perhaps he usually does. In my own case, however, I must
confess that I came into the theater unexpectedly, without preparation,
and stayed in it because I had a certain amount of rather accidental
success. It was not until after I had fumbled my way through a good
many successes and an appalling number of failures that I began to
doubt the sufficiency of dramatic instinct and to wonder whether or not
there were general laws governing dramatic structure which so poor a
head for theory as my own might grasp and use. I had read the *Poetics*
long before I tried playwriting, and I had looked doubtfully into a few
well-known handbooks on dramatic structure, but the maxims and theories propounded always drifted by me in a luminous haze — brilliant,
true, profound in context, yet quite without meaning for me when I considered the plan for a play or tried to clarify an emotion in dialogue. So
far as I could make out every play was a new problem, and the old rules
were inapplicable. There were so many rules, so many landmarks, so

many pitfalls, so many essential reckonings, that it seemed impossible to find your way through the jungle except by plunging ahead, trusting to your sense of direction and keeping your wits about you as you went.

But as the seasons went by and my failures fell as regularly as the leaves in autumn I began to search again among the theorists of the past for a word of wisdom that might take some of the gamble out of play-writing. What I needed most of all, I felt, was a working definition of what a play is, or perhaps a formula which would include all the elements necessary to a play structure. A play is almost always, probably, an attempt to recapture a vision for the stage. But when you are working in the theater it's most unsatisfactory to follow the gleam without a compass, quite risky to trust "the light that never was on sea or land" without making sure beforehand that you are not being led straight into a slough of despond. In other words you must make a choice among visions, and you must check your chosen vision carefully before assuming that it will make a play. But by what rules, what maps, what fields of reference can you check so intangible a substance as a revelation, a dream, an inspiration, or any similar nudge from the subconscious mind?

I shan't trouble you with the details of my search for a criterion, partly because I can't remember it in detail. But I reread Aristotle's *Poetics* in the light of some bitter experience, and one of his observations led me to a comparison of ancient and modern playwriting methods. In discussing construction he made a point of the recognition scene as essential to tragedy. The recognition scene, as Aristotle isolated it in the tragedies of the Greeks, was generally an artificial device, a central scene in which the leading character saw through a disguise, recognized as a friend or as an enemy, perhaps as a lover or a member of his own family, some person whose identity had been hidden. Iphigeneia, for example, acting as priestess in an alien country, receives a victim for sacrifice and then recognizes her own brother in this victim. There is an instant and profound emotional reaction, instantly her direction in the play is altered. But occasionally, in the greatest of the plays, the recognition turned on a situation far more convincing, though no less contrived. Oedipus, hunting savagely for the criminal who has brought the plague upon Thebes, discovers that he is himself that criminal — and since this is a discovery that affects not only the physical well-being and happiness of the hero, but the whole structure of his life, the effect on him and on the direction of the story is incalculably greater than could result from the more superficial revelation made to Iphigeneia.

Now scenes of exactly this sort are rare in the modern drama except in detective stories adapted for the stage. But when I probed a little more deeply into the memorable pieces of Shakespeare's theater and our own I began to see that though modern recognition scenes are subtler and harder to find, they are none the less present in the plays we choose to remember. They seldom have to do with anything so naïve as disguise or the unveiling of a personal identity. But the element of discovery is just as important as ever. For the mainspring in the mechanism of a modern play is almost invariably a discovery by the hero of some element in his environment or in his own soul of which he has not been aware — or which he has not taken sufficiently into account. Moreover, nearly every teacher of playwriting has had some inkling of this, though it was not until after I had worked out my own theory that what they said on this point took on accurate meaning for me. I still think that the rule which I formulated for my own guidance is more concise than any other, and so I give it here: A play should lead up to and away from a central crisis, and this crisis should consist in a discovery by the leading character which has an indelible effect on his thought and emotion and completely alters his course of action. The leading character, let me say again, must make the discovery; it must affect him emotionally; and it must alter his direction in the play.

Try that formula on any play you think worthy of study, and you will find that, with few exceptions, it follows this pattern or some variation of this pattern. The turning point of *The Green Pastures,* for example, is the discovery by God, who is the leading character, that a God who is to endure must conform to the laws of change. The turning point of *Hamlet* is Hamlet's discovery, in the play scene, that his uncle was unquestionably the murderer of his father. In *Abe Lincoln in Illinois* Lincoln's discovery is that he has been a coward, that he has stayed out of the fight for the Union because he was afraid. In each case, you will note, the discovery has a profound emotional effect on the hero, and gives an entirely new direction to his action in the play.

I'm not writing a disquisition on playwriting and wouldn't be competent to write one, but I do want to make a point of the superlative usefulness of this one touchstone for play structure. When a man sets out to write a play his first problem is his subject and the possibilities of that subject as a story to be projected from the stage. His choice of subject matter is his personal problem, and one that takes its answer from his personal relation to his times. But if he wants to know a possible play subject when he finds it, if he wants to know how to mold the subject into play form after he has found it, I doubt that he'll ever discover another standard as satisfactory as the modern version of Aristotle which I have suggested. If the plot he has in mind does not contain a playable episode in which the hero or heroine makes an emotional discovery, a discovery that practically dictates the end of the story, then such an episode must be inserted — and if no place can be found for it the subject is almost certainly a poor one for the theater. If this emotional discovery is contained in the story, but is not central, then it must be made central, and the whole action must revolve around it. In a three-act play it should fall near the end of the second act, though it may be delayed till the last; in a five-act play it will usually be found near the end of the third, though here also it can be delayed. Everything else in the play should be subordinated to this one episode — should lead up to or away from it.

Now this prime rule has a corollary which is just as important as the rule itself. The hero who is to make the central discovery in a play must not be a perfect man. He must have some variation of what Aristotle calls a tragic fault; and the reason he must have it is that when he makes his discovery he must change both in himself and in his action — and he must change for the better. The fault can be a very simple one — a mere unawareness, for example — but if he has no fault he cannot change for the better, but only for the worse, and for a reason which I shall discuss later, it is necessary that he must become more admirable, and not less so, at the end of the play. In other words, a hero must pass through an experience which opens his eyes to an error of his own. He must learn through suffering. In a tragedy he suffers death itself as a consequence of his fault or his attempt to correct it, but before he dies he has become a nobler person because of his recognition of his fault and the consequent alteration of his course of action. In a serious play which does not end in death he suffers a lesser punishment, but the pattern remains the same. In both forms he has a fault to begin with, he discovers that fault during the course of the action, and he does what he can to rectify it at the end. In *The Green Pastures* God's fault was that he believed himself perfect. He discovered that he was not perfect, that he had been in error and must make amends. Hamlet's fault was that he could not make up his mind to act. He offers many excuses for his indecision until he discovers that there is no real reason for hesitation and that he has delayed out of cowardice. Lincoln, in *Abe Lincoln in Illinois,* has exactly the same difficulty. In the climactic scene it is revealed to him that he had hesitated to take sides through fear of the consequences to himself, and he then chooses to go ahead without regard for what may be in store for him. From the point of view of the playwright, then, the essence of a tragedy, or even of a serious play, is the spiritual awakening, or regeneration, of his hero.

When a playwright attempts to reverse the formula, when his hero makes a discovery which has an evil effect, or one which the audience interprets as evil, on his character, the play is inevitably a failure on the stage. In *Troilus and Cressida* Troilus discovers that Cressida is a light woman. He draws from her defection the inference that all women are faithless — that faith in woman is the possession of fools. As a conse-

quence he turns away from life and seeks death in a cause as empty as
the love he has given up, the cause of the strumpet Helen. All the glory
of Shakespeare's verse cannot rescue the play for an audience, and save
in *Macbeth* Shakespeare nowhere wrote so richly, so wisely, or with such
a flow of brilliant metaphor.

For the audience will always insist that the alteration in the hero be
for the better — or for what it believes to be the better. As audiences
change the standards of good and evil change, though slowly and unpre-
dictably, and the meanings of plays change with the centuries. One
thing only is certain: that an audience watching a play will go along
with it only when the leading character responds in the end to what it
considers a higher moral impulse than moved him at the beginning of
the story, though the audience will of course define morality as it pleases
and in the terms of its own day. It may be that there is no absolute up or
down in this world, but the race believes that there is, and will not hear
of any denial.

And now at last I come to the point toward which I've been struggling so laboriously. Why does the audience come to the theater to look
on while an imaginary hero is put to an imaginary trial and comes out
of it with credit to the race and to himself? It was this question that
prompted my essay, and unless I've been led astray by my own predi-
lections there is a very possible answer in the rules for playwriting which
I have just cited. The theater originated in two complementary religious
ceremonies, one celebrating the animal in man and one celebrating the
god. Old Greek Comedy was dedicated to the spirits of lust and riot and
earth, spirits which are certainly necessary to the health and continuance
of the race. Greek tragedy was dedicated to man's aspiration, to his kinship with the gods, to his unending, blind attempt to lift himself above
his lusts and his pure animalism into a world where there are other values
than pleasure and survival. However unaware of it we may be, our
theater has followed the Greek patterns with no change in essence, from
Aristophanes and Euripides to our own day. Our more ribald musical
comedies are simply our approximation of the Bacchic rites of Old
Comedy. In the rest of our theater we sometimes follow Sophocles,
whose tragedy is always an exaltation of the human spirit, sometimes
Euripides, whose tragicomedy follows the same pattern of an excellence
achieved through suffering. The forms of both tragedy and comedy have
changed a good deal in nonessentials, but in essentials — and especially
in the core of meaning which they must have for audiences — they are
in the main the same religious rites which grew up around the altars of
Attica long ago.

It is for this reason that when you write for the theater you must
choose between your version of a phallic revel and your vision of what

mankind may or should become. Your vision may be faulty, or shallow, or sentimental, but it must conform to some aspiration in the audience, or the audience will reject it. Old Comedy, the celebration of the animal in us, still has a place in our theater, as it had in Athens, but here, as there, that part of the theater which celebrated man's virtue and his regeneration in hours of crisis is accepted as having the more important function. Our comedy is largely the Greek New Comedy, which grew out of Euripides' tragicomedy, and is separated from tragedy only in that it presents a happier scene and puts its protagonist through an ordeal which is less than lethal.

And since our plays, aside from those which are basically Old Comedy, are exaltations of the human spirit, since that is what an audience expects when it comes to the theater, the playwright gradually discovers, as he puts plays before audiences, that he must follow the ancient Aristotelian rule: he must build his plot around a scene wherein his hero discovers some mortal frailty or stupidity in himself and faces life armed with a new wisdom. He must so arrange his story that it will prove to the audience that men pass through suffering purified, that, animal though we are, despicable though we are in many ways, there is in us all some divine, incalculable fire that urges us to be better than we are.

It could be argued that what the audience demands of a hero is only conformity to race morality, to the code which seems to the spectators most likely to make for race survival. In many cases, especially in comedy, and obviously in the comedy of Molière, this is true. But in the majority of ancient and modern plays it seems to me that what the audience wants to believe is that men have a desire to break the molds of earth which encase them and claim a kinship with a higher morality than that which hems them in. The rebellion of Antigone, who breaks the laws of men through adherence to a higher law of affection, the rebellion of Prometheus, who breaks the law of the gods to bring fire to men, the rebellion of God in *The Green Pastures* against the rigid doctrine of the Old Testament, the rebellion of Tony in *They Knew What They Wanted* against the convention that called on him to repudiate his cuckold child, the rebellion of Liliom against the heavenly law which asked him to betray his own integrity and make a hypocrisy of his affection, even the repudiation of the old forms and the affirmation of new by the heroes of Ibsen and Shaw, these are all instances to me of the groping of men toward an excellence dimly apprehended, seldom possible of definition. They are evidence to me that the theater at its best is a religious affirmation, an age-old rite restating and reassuring man's belief in his own destiny and his ultimate hope. The theater is much older than the doctrine of evolution, but its one faith, asseverated again and again for every age and every year, is a faith in evolution, in the reaching and the climb of men toward distant goals, glimpsed but never seen, perhaps never achieved, or achieved only to be passed impatiently on the way to a more distant horizon.

tennessee williams

FOREWORD TO *CAMINO REAL*

It is amazing and frightening how completely one's whole being becomes absorbed in the making of a play. It is almost as if you were frantically constructing another world while the world that you live in dissolves beneath your feet, and that your survival depends on completing this construction at least one second before the old habitation collapses.

More than any other work that I have done, this play has seemed to me like the construction of another world, a separate existence. Of course, it is nothing more nor less than my conception of the time and world that I live in, and its people are mostly archetypes of certain basic attitudes and qualities with those mutations that would occur if they had continued along the road to this hypothetical terminal point in it.

A convention of the play is existence outside of time in a place of no specific locality. If you regard it that way, I suppose it becomes an elaborate allegory, but in New Haven we opened directly across the street from a movie theatre that was showing *Peter Pan* in Technicolor and it did not seem altogether inappropriate to me. Fairy tales nearly always have some simple moral lesson of good and evil, but that is not the secret of their fascination any more, I hope, than the philosophical import that might be distilled from the fantasies of *Camino Real* is the principal element of its appeal.

To me the appeal of this work is its unusual degree of freedom. When it began to get under way I felt a new sensation of release, as if I could "ride out" like a tenor sax taking the breaks in a Dixieland combo or a piano in a bop session. You may call it self-indulgence, but I was not doing it merely for myself. I could not have felt a purely private thrill of release unless I had hope of sharing this experience with lots and lots of audiences to come.

My desire was to give these audiences my own sense of something wild and unrestricted that ran like water in the mountains, or clouds changing shape in a gale, or the continually dissolving and transforming images of a dream. This sort of freedom is not chaos nor anarchy. On the contrary, it is the result of painstaking design, and in this work I have given more conscious attention to form and construction than I have in any work before. Freedom is not achieved simply by working freely.

Elia Kazan was attracted to this work mainly, I believe, for the same reason — its freedom and mobility of form. I know that we have kept saying the word "flight" to each other as if the play were merely an abstraction of the impulse to fly, and most of the work out of town, his in staging, mine in cutting and revising, has been with this impulse in mind: the achievement of a continual flow. Speech after speech and bit after bit that were nice in themselves have been remorselessly blasted out of the script and its staging wherever they seemed to obstruct or divert this flow.

There have been plenty of indications already that this play will exasperate and confuse a certain number of people which we hope is not so large as the number it is likely to please. At each performance a number of people have stamped out of the auditorium, with little regard for those whom they have had to crawl over, almost as if the building had caught on fire, and there have been sibilant noises on the way out and demands for money back if the cashier was foolish enough to remain in his box.

I am at a loss to explain this phenomenon, and if I am being facetious about one thing, I am being quite serious about another when I say that I had never for one minute supposed that the play would seem obscure and confusing to anyone who was willing to meet it even less than halfway. It was a costly production, and for this reason I had to read it aloud, together with a few of the actors on one occasion, before large groups of prospective backers, before the funds to produce it were in the till. It was only then that I came up against the disconcerting surprise that some people would think that the play needed clarification.

My attitude is intransigent. I still don't agree that it needs any explanation. Some poet has said that a poem should not mean but be. Of course, a play is not a poem, not even a poetic play has quite the same license as a poem. But to go to *Camino Real* with the inflexible demands of a logician is unfair to both parties.

In Philadelphia a young man from a literary periodical saw the play and then cross-examined me about all its dream-like images. He had made a list of them while he watched the play, and afterward at my hotel he brought out the list and asked me to explain the meaning of each one. I can't deny that I use a lot of those things called symbols but being a self-defensive creature, I say that symbols are nothing but the natural speech of drama.

We all have in our conscious and unconscious minds a great vocabulary of images, and I think all human communication is based on these images as are our dreams; and a symbol in a play has only one legitimate purpose which is to say a thing more directly and simply and beautifully than it could be said in words.

I hate writing that is a parade of images for the sake of images; I hate it so much that I close a book in disgust when it keeps on saying one thing is like another; I even get disgusted with poems that make nothing but comparisons between one thing and another. But I repeat that symbols, when used respectfully, are the purest language of plays. Sometimes it would take page after tedious page of exposition to put across an idea that can be said with an object or a gesture on the lighted stage.

To take one case in point: the battered portmanteau of Jacques Casanova is hurled from the balcony of a luxury hotel when his remittance check fails to come through. While the portmanteau is still in the air, he shouts: "Careful, I have — " — and when it has crashed to the street he continues — "fragile — mementoes. . ." I suppose that is a symbol, at least it is an object used to express as directly and vividly as possible certain things which could be said in pages of dull talk.

As for those patrons who departed before the final scene, I offer myself this tentative bit of solace: that these theatregoers may be a little domesticated in their theatrical tastes. A cage represents security as well as confinement to a bird that has grown used to being in it; and when a theatrical work kicks over the traces with such apparent insouciance, security seems challenged and, instead of participating in its sense of freedom, one out of a certain number of playgoers will rush back out to the more accustomed implausibility of the street he lives on.

To modify this effect of complaisance I would like to admit to you quite frankly that I can't say with any personal conviction that I have written a good play, I only know that I have felt a release in this work which I wanted you to feel with me.

arthur miller

FROM THE INTRODUCTION TO
ARTHUR MILLER'S COLLECTED PLAYS

I set out not to "write a tragedy" in this play [*Death of a Salesman*], but to show the truth as I saw it. However, some of the attacks upon it as a pseudo-tragedy contain ideas so misleading, and in some cases so laughable, that it might be in place here to deal with a few of them.

Aristotle having spoken of a fall from the heights, it goes without saying that someone of the common mold cannot be a fit tragic hero. It is now many centuries since Aristotle lived. There is no more reason for falling down in a faint before his *Poetics* than before Euclid's geometry, which has been amended numerous times by men with new insights; nor, for that matter, would I choose to have my illnesses diagnosed by Hippocrates rather than the most ordinary graduate of an American medical school, despite the Greek's genius. Things do change, and even a genius is limited by his time and the nature of his society.

I would deny, on grounds of simple logic, this one of Aristotle's contentions if only because he lived in a slave society. When a vast number of people are divested of alternatives, as slaves are, it is rather inevitable that one will not be able to imagine drama, let alone tragedy, as being possible for any but the higher ranks of society. There is a legitimate question of stature here, but none of rank, which is so often confused with it. So long as the hero may be said to have had alternatives of a magnitude to have materially changed the course of his life, it seems to me that in this respect at least, he cannot be debarred from the heroic role.

The question of rank is significant to me only as it reflects the question of the social application of the hero's career. There is no doubt that if a character is shown on the stage who goes through the most ordinary actions, and is suddenly revealed to be the President of the United States, his actions immediately assume a much greater magnitude, and pose the possibilities of much greater meaning, than if he is the corner grocer. But at the same time, his stature as a hero is not so utterly dependent upon his rank that the corner grocer cannot outdistance him as a tragic

From Introduction by the author to *Arthur Miller's Collected Plays*. Copyright © 1957 by Arthur Miller. Reprinted by permission of The Viking Press, Inc. and Elaine Green, Ltd.

figure — providing, of course, that the grocer's career engages the issues of, for instance, the survival of the race, the relationships of man to God — the questions, in short, whose answers define humanity and the right way to live so that the world is a home, instead of a battleground or a fog in which disembodied spirits pass each other in an endless twilight.

In this respect *Death of a Salesman* is a slippery play to categorize because nobody in it stops to make a speech objectively stating the great issues which I believe it embodies. If it were a worse play, less closely articulating its meanings with its actions, I think it would have more quickly satisfied a certain kind of criticism. But it was meant to be less a play than a fact; it refused admission to its author's opinions and opened itself to a revelation of process and the operations of an ethic, of social laws of action no less powerful in their effects upon individuals than any tribal law administered by gods with names. I need not claim that this play is a genuine solid gold tragedy for my opinions on tragedy to be held valid. My purpose here is simply to point out a historical fact which must be taken into account in any consideration of tragedy, and it is the sharp alteration in the meaning of rank in society between the present time and the distant past. More important to me is the fact that this particular kind of argument obscures much more relevant considerations.

One of these is the question of intensity. It matters not at all whether a modern play concerns itself with a grocer or a president if the intensity of the hero's commitment to his course is less than the maximum possible. It matters not at all whether the hero falls from a great height or a small one, whether he is highly conscious or only dimly aware of what is happening, whether his pride brings the fall or an unseen pattern written behind clouds; if the intensity, the human passion to surpass his given bounds, the fanatic insistence upon his self-conceived role — if these are not present there can only be an outline of tragedy but no living thing. I believe, for myself, that the lasting appeal of tragedy is due to our need to face the fact of death in order to strengthen ourselves for life, and that over and above this function of the tragic viewpoint there are and will be a great number of formal variations which no single definition will ever embrace.

Another issue worth considering is the so-called tragic victory, a question closely related to the consciousness of the hero. One makes nonsense of this if a "victory" means that the hero makes us feel some certain joy when, for instance, he sacrifices himself for a "cause," and unhappy and morose because he dies without one. To begin at the bottom, a man's death is and ought to be an essentially terrifying thing and ought to make nobody happy. But in a great variety of ways even death, the ultimate negative, can be, and appear to be, an assertion of bravery, and can serve to separate the death of man from the death of animals; and I think it is this distinction which underlies any conception of a victory in death. For a society of faith, the nature of the death can prove the existence of the spirit, and posit its immortality. For a secular society it is perhaps more difficult for such a victory to document itself and to make itself felt, but, conversely, the need to offer greater proofs of the humanity of man can make that victory more real. It goes without saying that in a society where there is basic disagreement as to the right way to live, there can hardly be agreement as to the right way to die, and both life and death must be heavily weighted with meaningless futility.

It was not out of any deference to a tragic definition that Willy Loman is filled with a joy, however broken-hearted, as he approaches his end, but simply that my sense of his character dictated his joy, and even what I felt was an exultation. In terms of his character, he has achieved a very powerful piece of knowledge, which is that he is loved by his son and has been embraced by him and forgiven. In this he is given his existence, so to speak — his fatherhood, for which he has always striven and which until now he could not achieve. That he is unable to take this victory thoroughly to his heart, that it closes the circle for him and propels him to his death, is the wage of his sin, which was to have committed himself so completely to the counterfeits of dignity and the false coinage embodied in his idea of success that he can prove his existence only by bestowing "power" on his posterity, a power deriving from the sale of his last asset, himself, for the price of his insurance policy.

I must confess here to a miscalculation, however. I did not realize while writing the play that so many people in the world do not see as clearly, or would not admit, as I thought they must, how futile most lives are; so there could be no hope of consoling the audience for the death of this man. I did not realize either how few would be impressed by the fact that this man is actually a very brave spirit who cannot settle for half but must pursue his dream of himself to the end. Finally, I thought it must be clear, even obvious, that this was no dumb brute heading mindlessly to his catastrophe.

I have no need to be Willy's advocate before the jury which decides who is and who is not a tragic hero. I am merely noting that the lingering ponderousness of so many ancient definitions has blinded students and critics to the facts before them, and not only in regard to this play. Had Willy been unaware of his separation from values that endure he would have died contentedly while polishing his car, probably on a Sunday afternoon with the ball game coming over the radio. But he was agonized by his awareness of being in a false position, so constantly haunted by the hollowness of all he had placed his faith in, so aware, in short, that he must somehow be filled in his spirit or fly apart, that he

staked his very life on the ultimate assertion. That he had not the intellectual fluency to verbalize his situation is not the same thing as saying
that he lacked awareness, even an overly intensified consciousness that
the life he had made was without form and inner meaning.

To be sure, had he been able to know that he was as much the
victim of his beliefs as their defeated exemplar, had he known how
much of guilt he ought to bear and how much to shed from his soul, he
would be more conscious. But it seems to me that there is of necessity
a severe limitation of self-awareness in any character, even the most
knowing, which serves to define him as a character, and more, that this
very limit serves to complete the tragedy and, indeed, to make it at all
possible. Complete consciousness is possible only in a play about forces,
like *Prometheus,* but not in a play about people. I think that the point
is whether there is a sufficient awareness in the hero's career to make the
audience supply the rest. Had Oedipus, for instance, been more conscious and more aware of the forces at work upon him he must surely
have said that he was not really to blame for having cohabited with his
mother since neither he nor anyone else knew she was his mother. He
must surely decide to divorce her, provide for their children, firmly resolve
to investigate the family background of his next wife, and thus deprive
us of a very fine play and the name for a famous neurosis. But he is
conscious only up to a point, the point at which guilt begins. Now he is
inconsolable and must tear out his eyes. What is tragic about this? Why
is it not even ridiculous? How can we respect a man who goes to such
extremities over something he could in no way help or prevent? The answer, I think, is not that we respect the man, but that we respect the
Law he has so completely broken, wittingly or not, for it is that Law
which, we believe, defines us as men. The confusion of some critics view-
ing *Death of a Salesman* in this regard is that they do not see that Willy
Loman has broken a law without whose protection life is insupportable
if not incomprehensible to him and to many others; it is the law which
says that a failure in society and in business has no right to live. Unlike
the law against incest, the law of success is not administered by statute
or church, but it is very nearly as powerful in its grip upon men. The
confusion increases because, while it is a law, it is by no means a wholly
agreeable one even as it is slavishly obeyed, for to fail is no longer to
belong to society, in his estimate. Therefore, the path is opened for those
who wish to call Willy merely a foolish man even as they themselves are
living in obedience to the same law that killed him. Equally, the fact
that Willy's law — the belief, in other words, which administers guilt to
him — is not a civilizing statute whose destruction menaces us all; it is,
rather, a deeply believed and deeply suspect "good" which, when ques-
tioned as to its value, as it is in this play, serves more to raise our anxieties

than to reassure us of the existence of an unseen but humane metaphysical system in the world. My attempt in the play was to counter this
anxiety with an opposing system which, so to speak, is in a race for
Willy's faith, and it is the system of love which is the opposite of the law
of success. It is embodied in Biff Loman, but by the time Willy can per-
ceive his love it can serve only as an ironic comment upon the life he
sacrificed for power and for success and its tokens.

edward albee

WHICH THEATRE IS THE ABSURD ONE?

A theatre person of my acquaintance — a man whose judgment must
be respected, though more for the infallibility of his intuition than for
his reasoning — remarked just the other week, "The Theatre of the Absurd
has had it; it's on its way out; it's through."

Now this, on the surface of it, seems to be a pretty funny attitude
to be taking toward a theatre movement which has, only in the past
couple of years, been impressing itself on the American public consciousness. Or is it? Must we judge that a theatre of such plays as Samuel
Beckett's "Krapp's Last Tape," Jean Genet's "The Balcony" (both long,
long runners off-Broadway) and Eugene Ionesco's "Rhinoceros" — which,
albeit in a hoked-up production, had a substantial season *on* Broadway —
has been judged by the theatre public and found wanting?

And shall we have to assume that The Theatre of the Absurd Reper-
tory Company, currently playing at New York's off-Broadway Cherry
Lane Theatre — presenting works by Beckett, Ionesco, Genet, Arrabal,
Jack Richardson, Kenneth Koch and myself — being the first such collective representation of the movement in the United States, is also a kind
of farewell to the movement? For that matter, just what *is* The Theatre
of the Absurd?

Well, let me come at it obliquely. When I was told, about a year
ago, that I was considered a member in good standing of The Theatre of
the Absurd I was deeply offended. I was deeply offended because I had

New York Times Magazine, February 25, 1962, pp. 30, 31, 64, 66. © 1962 by The New
York Times Company. Reprinted by the kind permission of Edward Albee.

never heard the term before and I immediately assumed that it applied to the theatre uptown — Broadway.

What (I was reasoning to myself) could be more absurd than a theatre in which the esthetic criterion is something like this: A "good" play is one which makes money; a "bad" play (in the sense of "Naughty! Naughty!" I guess) is one which does not; a theatre in which performers have plays rewritten to correspond to the public relations image of themselves; a theatre in which playwrights are encouraged (what a funny word!) to think of themselves as little cogs in a great big wheel; a theatre in which imitation has given way to imitation of imitation; a theatre in which London "hits" are willy-nilly, in a kind of reverse of chauvinism, greeted in a manner not unlike a colony's obeisance to the Crown; a theatre in which real estate owners and theatre party managements predetermine the success of unknown quantities; a theatre in which everybody scratches and bites for billing as though it meant access to the last bomb shelter on earth; a theatre in which, in a given season, there was not a single performance of a play by Beckett, Brecht, Chekhov, Genet, Ibsen, O'Casey, Pirandello, Shaw, Strindberg — or Shakespeare? What, indeed, I thought, could be more absurd than that? (My conclusions . . . obviously.)

For it emerged that The Theatre of the Absurd, aside from being the title of an excellent book by Martin Esslin on what is loosely called the avant-garde theatre, was a somewhat less than fortunate catch-all phrase to describe the philosophical attitudes and theatre methods of a number of Europe's finest and most adventurous playwrights and their followers.

I was less offended, but still a little dubious. Simply: I don't like labels; they can be facile and can lead to non-think on the part of the public. And unless it is understood that the playwrights of The Theatre of the Absurd represent a group only in the sense that they seem to be doing something of the same thing in vaguely similar ways at approximately the same time — unless this is understood, then the labeling itself will be more absurd than the label.

Playwrights, by nature, are grouchy, withdrawn, envious, greedy, suspicious and, in general, quite nice people — and the majority of them wouldn't be caught dead in a colloquy remotely resembling the following:

IONESCO
(At a Left Bank cafe table, spying Beckett and Genet strolling past in animated conversation)
Hey! Sam! Jean!

GENET
Hey, it's Eugene! Sam, it's Eugene!

BECKETT

Well, I'll be damned. Hi there, Eugene boy.

IONESCO

Sit down, kids.

GENET

Sure thing.

IONESCO
(*Rubbing his hands together*)
Well, what's new in The Theate of the Absurd?

BECKETT
Oh, less than a lot of people think. (*They all laugh.*)

Etc. No. Not very likely. Get a playwright alone sometime, get a few drinks in him, and maybe he'll be persuaded to sound off about his "intention" and the like — and hate himself for it the next day. But put a group of playwrights together in a room, and the conversation — if there is any — will, more likely than not, concern itself with sex, restaurants and the movies.

Very briefly, then — and reluctantly, because I am a playwright and would much rather talk about sex, restaurants and the movies — and stumblingly, because I do not pretend to understand it entirely, I will try to define The Theatre of the Absurd. As I get it, The Theatre of the Absurd is an absorption-in-art of certain existentialist and post-existentialist philosophical concepts having to do, in the main, with man's attempts to make sense for himself out of his senseless position in a world which makes no sense — which makes no sense because the moral, religious, political and social structures man has erected to "illusion" himself have collapsed.

Albert Camus put it this way: "A world that can be explained by reasoning, however faulty, is a familiar world. But in a universe that is suddenly deprived of illusions and of light, man feels a stranger. His is an irremediable exile, because he is deprived of memories of a lost homeland as much as he lacks the hope of a promised land to come. This divorce between man and his life, the actor and his setting, truly constitutes the feeling of Absurdity."

And Eugene Ionesco says this: "Absurd is that which is devoid of purpose. . . . Cut off from his religious metaphysical, and transcendental roots, man is lost; all his actions become senseless, absurd, useless."

And to sum up the movement, Martin Esslin writes, in his book "The Theatre of the Absurd": "Ultimately, a phenomenon like The Theatre of the Absurd does not reflect despair or a return to dark irrational forces but expresses modern man's endeavor to come to terms with the world in which he lives. It attempts to make him face up to the human condition as it really is, to free him from illusions that are bound to cause constant maladjustment and disappointment. . . . For the dignity of man lies in his ability to face reality in all its senselessness; to accept it freely, without fear, without illusions — and to laugh at it."

Amen.

(And while we're on the subject of Amen, one wearies of the complaint that The Theatre of the Absurd playwrights alone are having at God these days. The notion that God is dead, indifferent, or insane — a notion blasphemous, premature, or academic depending on your persuasion — while surely a tenet of some of the playwrights under discussion, is, it seems to me, of a piece with Mr. Tennessee Williams' description of the Deity, in "The Night of the Iguana," as "a senile delinquent.")

So much for the attempt to define terms. Now, what of this theatre? What of this theatre in which, for example, a legless old couple live out their lives in twin ashcans, surfacing occasionally for food or conversation (Samuel Beckett's "Endgame"); in which a man is seduced, and rather easily, by a girl with three well-formed and functioning noses (Eugene Ionesco's "Jack, or The Submission"); in which, on the same stage, one group of Negro actors is playing at pretending to be white, and another group of Negro actors is playing at pretending to be Negro (Jean Genet's "The Blacks")?

What of this theatre? Is it, as it has been accused of being, obscure, sordid, destructive, anti-theatre, perverse and absurd (in the sense of foolish)? Or is it merely, as I have so often heard it put, that, "This sort of stuff is too depressing, too . . . too mixed-up; I go to the theatre to relax and have a good time."

I would submit that it is this latter attitude — that the theatre is a place to relax and have a good time — in conflict with the purpose of The Theatre of the Absurd — which is to make a man face up to the human condition as it really is — that has produced all the brouhaha and the dissent. I would submit that The Theatre of the Absurd, in the sense that it is truly the contemporary theatre, facing as it does man's condition as it is, is the Realistic theatre of our time; and that the supposed Realistic theatre — the term used here to mean most of what is done on Broadway — in the sense that it panders to the public need for self-congratulation and reassurance and presents a false picture of ourselves to ourselves is, with an occasional very lovely exception, really and truly The Theatre of the Absurd.

And I would submit further that the health of a nation, a society, can be determined by the art it demands. We have insisted of television and our movies that they not have anything to do with anything, that they be our never-never land; and if we demand this same function of our live theatre, what will be left of the visual-auditory arts — save the dance (in which nobody talks) and music (to which nobody listens)?

It has been my fortune, the past two or three years, to travel around a good deal, in pursuit of my career — Berlin, London, Buenos Aires, for example; and I have discovered a couple of interesting things. I have discovered that audiences in these and other major cities demand of their commercial theatre — and get — a season of plays in which the froth and junk are the exception and not the rule. To take a case: in Berlin, in 1959, Adamov, Genet, Beckett and Brecht (naturally) were playing the big houses; this past fall, Beckett again, Genet again, Pinter twice, etc. To take another case: in Buenos Aires there are over a hundred experimental theatres.

These plays cannot be put on in Berlin over the head of a protesting or an indifferent audience; these experimental theatres cannot exist in Buenos Aires without subscription. In the end — and it must always come down to this, no matter what other failings a theatre may have — in the end a public will get what it deserves, and no better.

I have also discovered, in my wanderings, that young people throng to what is new and fresh in the theatre. Happily, this holds true in the United States as well. At the various colleges I have gone to to speak I have found an eager, friendly and knowledgeable audience, an audience which is as dismayed by the Broadway scene as any proselytizer for the avant-garde. I have found among young people an audience which is not so preconditioned by pap as to have cut off half of its responses. (It is interesting to note, by the way, that if an off-Broadway play has a substantial run, its audiences will begin young and grow older as the run goes on, cloth often give way to furs, walkers and subway riders to taxi-takers. Exactly the opposite is true on Broadway.)

The young, of course, are always questioning values knocking the status quo about considering shibboleths to see if they are pronounceable. In time, it is to be regretted, most of them — the kids — will settle down to their own version of the easy, the standard; but in the meanwhile . . . in the meanwhile they are a wonderful, alert, alive, accepting audience.

And I would go so far as to say that it is the responsibility of everyone who pretends any interest at all in the theatre to get up off their six-ninety seats and find out what the theatre is really about. For it is a lazy public which produces a slothful and irresponsible theatre.

Now, I would suspect that my theatre-friend with the infallible intuition is probably right when he suggests that The Theatre of the Absurd (or the avant-garde theatre, or whatever you want to call it) as it now stands is on its way out. Or at least is undergoing change. All living organisms undergo constant change. And while it is certain that the nature of this theatre will remain constant, its forms, its methods — its devices, if you will — most necessarily will undergo mutation.

This theatre has no intention of running downhill; and the younger playwrights will make use of the immediate past and mould it to their own needs. (Harold Pinter, for example, could not have written "The Caretaker" had Samuel Beckett not existed, but Pinter is, nonetheless, moving in his own direction.) And it is my guess that the theatre in the United States will always hew more closely to the post-Ibsen/Chekhov tradition than does the theatre in France, let us say. It is our nature as a country, a society. But we will experiment, and we will expect your attention.

For just as it is true that our response to color and form was forever altered once the impressionist painters put their minds to canvas, it is just as true that the playwrights of The Theatre of the Absurd have forever altered our response to the theatre.

And one more point: The avant-garde theatre is fun; it is free-swinging, bold, iconoclastic and often wildly, wildly funny. If you will approach it with childlike innocence — putting your standard responses aside, for they do not apply — if you will approach it on its own terms, I think you will be in for a liberating surprise. I think you may no longer be content with plays that you can't remember halfway down the block. You will not only be doing yourself some good, but you will be having a great time, to boot. And even though it occurs to me that such a fine combination must be sinful, I still recommend it.

2   3   4   5   6   7   8   9   0